# THE PRAIRIE
# IN NINETEENTH-CENTURY
# AMERICAN POETRY

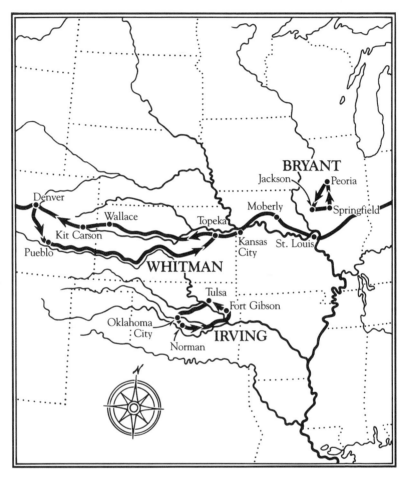

Routes traveled on the prairies and plains by Irving, Bryant, and Whitman. Irving's horseback tour in Oklahoma lasted about one month. Bryant's horseback tour in Illinois took five days. Whitman's train tour to Colorado lasted September through December 1879. (Map derived in part from maps in Irving's A *Tour on the Prairies* and Eitner's *Walt Whitman's Western Jaunt.*)

# THE PRAIRIE
# IN NINETEENTH-CENTURY
# AMERICAN POETRY

by Steven Olson

University of Oklahoma Press
Norman and London

Library of Congress Cataloging-in-Publication Data

Olson, Steven, 1950–
    The prairie in nineteenth-century American poetry / by Steven
Olson.
        p.   cm.
    Includes bibliographical references and index.
    ISBN 0–8061–2600–0 (alk. paper)
    1. American poetry—19th century—History and criticism.
    2. Prairies in literature. I. Title.
    PS310.P67048   1994
    811' .30932145—dc20                                    93–32550
                                                                CIP

Text design by Cathy Imboden.

The paper in this book meets the guidelines for permanence and durability
of the Committee on Production Guidelines for Book Longevity of the
Council on Library Resources, Inc. ∞

1   2   3   4   5   6   7   8   9   10

# CONTENTS

# PREFACE

This study traces images of the prairies and plains[1] in poetry written in English in the United States during the nineteenth century and describes the import of those images—how they depict and characterize the physical landscape, and how the poetic prairies and plains symbolically incorporate people, imagination, ideology, and place in the United States.

My first chapter suggests how images of the prairies and plains began to incorporate the expansionist ideology of America at the time and how perception helped to figuratively shape the landscape into metaphor. Two examples of exploration journals and travel books introduce the main images and themes associated with this landscape and demonstrate how it made its way into American literature.

In the second chapter I compare William Cullen Bryant's actual experience on the prairies, as revealed in his letters, with his poems about the prairies. His writings offer a unique insight into how the prairie landscape is figuratively shaped by a public voice into a national metaphor. Chapter 3 examines how other popular poets work the poetic ground that Bryant has broken in order to cultivate an optimistic metaphor.

Chapter 4 explores the failing of the optimistic metaphor in the private voices of Emily Dickinson and Herman Melville. Dickinson suggests that the prairie metaphor takes its meaning not from the landscape itself, nor from the cultural characteristics of America, but from the individual who creates the metaphor. Thinking similarly, Melville reshapes the metaphor, exposing its darker side, suggesting that there are weeds of spiritual and moral deterioration in the American garden.

Chapter 5 analyzes the synthesizing voice of Walt Whitman, which reconciles the private and public voices. Whitman's prairie metaphor asserts America's optimistic qualities and places the prairies and America centrally in a global context. Though Whitman's version of the metaphor is essentially optimistic, his poetic voice, besides being the best nineteenth-century American voice to use the prairie metaphor extensively, develops the metaphor the most fully to reap the full harvest of the poetic prairies.

Comparing the poetic metaphor to writings of nineteenth-century American historians, the final chapter substantiates the pervasiveness and ideological base of the metaphor and draws conclusions about the influence of an incipient democracy on poets and their poetry.

As these poets use the prairies and plains symbolically or metaphorically, an individual image of the prairies often calls up a complex of meanings.[2] I would like, therefore, to use Gaston Bachelard's definition of an image to explain how images of the prairies and plains affect the reader emotionally and to suggest that such images can function individually and collectively:

> The reverberations [of a poetic] image bring about a change of being. It is as though the poet's being were our being. . . .
>
> Through this reverberation, . . . we feel a poetic power rising naively within us. After the original reverberation, we are able to experience resonances, sentimental repercussions, reminders of our past. . . .
>
> We cease to consider [the poetic image] as an "object" but feel that the "objective" critical attitude stifles the "reverberation." . . .
>
> When I receive a new poetic image, I experience its quality of inter-subjectivity.

Specifically addressing "immensity," a primary quality of the space or openness of the prairie, Bachelard further describes the effect of such an open image on a reader: "In analyzing images of immensity, we should realize within ourselves the pure being of pure imagination . . . [because] immensity is within ourselves."[3]

While Bachelard's explanation nicely identifies how the meanings associated with the image are transferred and why they are so persistent, I disagree with him on an important point. He contends that "nothing prepares a poetic image, especially not culture." He speaks here from a phenomenological stance that is limited to the *"new* poetic image"—one entirely imaginative, created in the poet's mind, and that then needs to be incorporated by language. He does not intend to account for an established poetic image. I suggest that established images, like those of the prairies and plains in the nineteenth century, are internalized or imagined by the reader in the way Bachelard describes, but that the reverberations and resonances of such established images are in fact culturally created. Bachelard's description of the effect of an image on a reader—and I would add the effect of a symbol or metaphor—thus helps to explain the process by which a culturally significant image, like one associated with the prairie, is perpetuated by the literature of its culture.

Two early works of scholarship have made the study of the relationship between the prairies and literature possible and are indispensable to a student of prairie literature: Ralph Leslie Rusk's *The Literature of the Middle Western Frontier* (1925) and Dorothy Anne Dondore's *The Prairie and the Making of Middle America: Four Centuries of Description* (1926). Henry Nash Smith's *Virgin Land: The American West as Symbol and Myth* (1950) is the first serious work on the symbolic character of the American West, and Leo Marx's *The Machine in the Garden: Technology and the Pastoral Ideal in America* (1967) has also been an influential work for students of the relationship between literature and the land.

More recently Myra Jehlen and Annette Kolodny have examined the connections between land and literature and argue some points that provide a fruitful foreground. In *American Incarnation: The Individual, the Nation, and the Continent* (1986), Jehlen asserts the significance of the land to America, articulating a dynamic that also describes the relationship between the prairies and plains and nineteenth-century American poetry: "the decisive factor shaping the founding conceptions of 'America' and of 'the American' was material rather than conceptual; rather than a set of abstract ideas, the physical fact of the continent" (3). "When the liberal ideal fused with the material landscape, it produced an 'America' that was not allegory, for its meaning was not detachable, but symbol, its meaning inherent in its matter" (9). She notes another characteristic that is also a part of the poetic metaphor, the connection between the "continent's . . . physicality" and the metaphysical: "it is precisely because the concept of America is rooted in the physical finite that it can be infinitely metaphysical" (9).

Also suggesting the symbolic nature of the prairies, Kolodny's *The Land before Her: Fantasy and Experience of the American Frontier, 1630–1860* (1984) thoroughly examines the meanings imbued in the prairies by women writing in the nineteenth century. "The prairie," she writes, "spoke to women's fantasies. And there . . . the newly self-conscious American Eve proclaimed a paradise in which the garden and the home were one" (6). These fantasies were thwarted, remaining "only uncompleted mythic possibilities." Yet women novelists of the prairies "declared" that paradise "was now to be claimed by Adam and Eve alike. And a raw frontier might yet sustain viable images of home" (226).

More recently, Kolodny's article "Letting Go Our Grand Obsessions: Notes Toward a New Literary History of the American Frontier" (1992) argues the importance of the frontier to American literature. She asserts "that there always stands at the heart of frontier literature . . . a physical terrain," and that "the collisions and negotiations of distinct cultural groups" are "expressed" in the interaction of "languages and texts" (5). Her argument for a multicultural, multilingual, interdisciplinary approach is compelling: "My reformulation of the term 'frontier' comes to mean what we in the Southwest call *la frontera,* or the borderlands, that liminal landscape of changing meanings on which distinct human cultures first encounter one another's 'otherness' and appropriate, accommodate, or domesticate it through language" (9). My study, I hope, fits into this larger framework of literary history by focusing on one culture's view of a physical frontier as a means of defining itself and its literature.

I also owe personal debts. Emily Stipes Watts provided constant guidance and inspiration during the formative stages of this study. She, George Hendrick, and Charles Sanders each read versions of the manuscript and offered helpful advice. John Hallwas gave advice about Illinois poets. I thank Kimberly Wiar and Sarah Nestor of the University of Oklahoma Press for their courtesy and professional advice. This book is clearer than it might have been thanks to Larry Hamberlin's many useful suggestions about writing style.

Discussions with Ann were principal in forming many of the ideas in this study, and she read—and reread—this work in all its stages, making suggestions for changes at every level. With Ann, Carey and Cavan helped me to maintain my perspective—kept me joyous—at what would otherwise have been some desperate times.

I thank *North Dakota Quarterly* and *Western Illinois Regional Studies* for permission to reprint parts of articles. Some of the material about Bryant's letters from the prairies appeared in *NDQ,* and some of the material about Illinois poets appeared in *WIRS.* "The Gift Outright" by Robert Frost is also reprinted by permission.

STEVEN OLSON

*Ellensburg, Washington*

# THE PRAIRIE
# IN NINETEENTH-CENTURY
# AMERICAN POETRY

# CHAPTER ONE

# EXPLORING THE PRAIRIES

The land was ours before we were the land's.
She was our land more than a hundred years
Before we were her people. She was ours
In Massachusetts, in Virginia,
But we were England's, still colonials,
Possessing what we still were unpossessed by,
Possessed by what we now no more possessed.
Something we were withholding made us weak
Until we found out that it was ourselves
We were withholding from our land of living,
And forthwith found salvation in surrender.
Such as we were we gave ourselves outright
(The deed of gift was many deeds of war)
To the land vaguely realizing westward,
But still unstoried, artless, unenhanced,
Such as she was, such as she would become.

**Robert Frost,**
"The Gift Outright"

Robert Frost proclaims "outright" that human blood and bodies absorbed by the earth established a contract, a covenant, between the people of the United States and the continent. The

---

deed testified to compatriotism, worth, commitment, and salvation—it generated a "spirit of place." This dual bond—historical and sacrificial—was not a culmination, however, but a beginning. Symbolic makings—imaginative acts, literary and artful enhancements—would realize the new nation in the future.

The poetic treatment of the prairies and plains in the United States during the nineteenth century is such a symbolic making—one informed predominantly by a nationalist ideology like that expressed in Frost's poem, an ideology of expansionism, progressivism, and manifest destiny.[1]

The opening of the prairied frontier, which played a large part in displacing the Indians, was the dominant fact of American expansion and "progress" during the nineteenth century, and arguably, with the possible exception of the Civil War, the dominant fact of American history in that century.[2] The lands between the Appalachians and the Mississippi River were ceded by the states to the newly formed federal government between 1780 and 1802. The Louisiana Purchase, formalized on April 30, 1803, acquired the land between the Mississippi River and the Rocky Mountains—claiming prairies and plains for future white settlement early in the century. The area east of the Mississippi began to be settled around 1815. By 1840 the Mississippi Valley was no longer frontier, and by 1850 the Great Lakes Plains and Gulf Plains were no longer frontier (according to the census bureau's definition of *frontier*—not more than six persons per square mile). The settlement of the far western Great Plains began full force in 1870, and that area was no longer frontier in 1890.

The Mississippi was a main entrance into the prairied West, but other means of cheap transportation developed rapidly. The opening of the Erie Canal in 1825 led to something like a canal fever, which opened the lands around the Great Lakes for settlement. The number of steamboats to transport goods east and west on the Ohio and Mississippi rivers grew from 75 in 1825 to 187 in 1840. More expensive to build and maintain than canals, railroads were developed later, but by 1855 a web of railroads covered what is now Ohio, Indiana, and Illinois. By 1883 railroads reached from

Duluth, Minnesota, to Portland, Oregon; from Council Bluffs, Nebraska, to Sacramento, California; and from Dallas, Texas, to Los Angeles, California.

The development of the transportation system coincided with changes in land policy. The Land Act of 1800 maintained the two dollar per acre minimum purchase price, but reduced the minimum purchase from 640 to 320 acres and extended the term of credit from one to four years (though requiring a 25 percent down payment). The Land Act of 1804 again reduced the minimum purchase—to 160 acres. The Land Act of 1820 brought the minimum purchase down to 80 acres, the minimum purchase price to $1.25 per acre. By abolishing the credit system, however, the 1820 act also put certain constraints on prospective buyers, who nonetheless remained interested in cheap land. A later statute, the Homestead Act, also attests to the increasing interest in settling the prairied West. With this act, which was brought before Congress as early as 1846 but not voted into law until 1862, the prospect of free land was offered to any citizen or any alien declaring his intent to become a citizen. One hundred and sixty acres of land could be earned by proving that one had lived on it for five years and by paying a small title fee.

The tragic side of this expansion was the removal of American Indians from their lands. On January 27, 1825, President James Monroe brought before Congress a plan to remove the Indians in the East, and during the next fifteen years tribes—including the Choctaw, Cherokee, Shawnee, Delaware, Kickapoo, Sauk, Fox, and Chippewa, among others—were forced westward. By 1840 a Permanent Indian Frontier existed between the 95th and 101st meridians. The "permanent" frontier was intended to be the last removal of the Indians, but because the Indians already living there took a dislike to the eastern Indian "intruders" and because white settlers soon demanded more land, the idea of "One Big Reservation" gave way to "Concentration" and eventually to "Small Reservations" by 1875.[3] By 1875 the Indians had been moved to reservations that only dotted the half of the continent west of the Missouri River.

The traditional historical view has been that a national

"faith" in manifest destiny was the dominant motivator for this expansion. But the historian Richard White qualifies that notion, suggesting that such a view does not explain such significant historical events as the long refusal to annex Texas and the "bitter divisions" resulting from the Mexican War. White claims instead that "American expansion was not as much the outcome of a widely shared belief in manifest destiny as it was the compromised achievement of an incipient nationalism," which included "sectionalism and racism."[4]

Accepting White's qualification, we can see this nationalism, sectionalism, and racism in the poetic metaphor of the prairies and plains. At the same time, however, we can see in the metaphor other notions connected essentially with manifest destiny. Even if manifest destiny was not the sole motivator of American expansion, it is nonetheless a clearly identifiable historical concept, and in the poetic metaphor it is an essential informing principle. A term coined by the New York newspaperman John O'Sullivan, "manifest destiny" embraced the following essential notions, according to White: "Providence made the United States the [dominant figure] for this continent because of Providence's fondness for favoring liberty and self-government. . . . Before the claims of Providence, legal claims of other nations, let alone the unmentioned claims of Indians who actually lived on these lands, were mere 'cobweb tissues.'"[5]

The ideology suggested by this sketch of American expansion and manifest destiny is the foundation of the poetic metaphor of the prairies and plains. The metaphor initially made its way into the literature of the prairies and plains through journals of exploration, guidebooks, and travel books, in which images of the prairies and plains became conventionalized and publicized. Works like Meriwether Lewis's and William Clark's *History of the Expedition* (1814) and Washington Irving's *A Tour on the Prairies* (1835) helped generate an image and concept of the plains and prairies for the American reading public and tied that concept to the dominant ideology. The landscape, though sometimes forbidding, even destructive, was by and large depicted as inviting, receptive of white settlement. Described in these works, it appealed to such values as adventure and human progress.[6]

The prairies and plains figure prominently in the sections of Lewis and Clark's journals that describe their journey from St. Louis to the Rocky Mountains in order to chart the newly acquired Louisiana Territory between 1804 and 1806. With the first edition of their *History of the Expedition*, published by Nicholas Biddle in 1814, and with at least six other editions published between 1814 and 1842 (including German and Dutch editions), Lewis and Clark provided one of the earliest and most widely read descriptions of the prairies and plains for a nineteenth-century audience.[7]

From atop an Indian burial mound, they paint a characteristic picture of the prairies:

> A delightful prospect presented itself; the level and extensive meadows watered by the Nemahaw, and enlivened by the few trees and shrubs skirting the borders of the river and its tributary streams; the low land of the Missouri covered with undulating grass, nearly five feet high, gradually rising to a second plain, where rich weeds and flowers are interspersed with copses of the Osage plum; further back are seen small groves of trees; an abundance of grapes; the wild cherry of the Missouri, resembling our own, but larger, and growing on a small bush; and the choke-cherry. (*History* 1:43–44)

Other particulars describing the prairies are strewn throughout the history. Size is usually given in general terms, such as "vast" or "large," but once they estimate the length of a prairie as being "four or five miles" across (1:44). They name a prairie "Bald-pate" because of "a ridge of naked hills which bound it, running parallel with the river as far as we could see, at from three to six miles' distance" (1:47). A prairie is almost invariably "rich," "handsome," "fertile," or "beautiful." In one area the prairies "have the appearance of distinct farms, divided by narrow strips of woodland, which follow the borders of the small runs leading to the river" (1:40).

The flora and fauna also add to the description. In addition to flowers, grasses, Osage plums, grapes, cherries, and chokecherries, the prairies have "raspberries, wild apples, . . . mulberries," and "wild rye and a kind of wild potato" (1:32, 42, and passim). For animals the prairies have buffalo, dear, bear, wolves, hawks, skunks, elk, goats, grouse and larks (1:120, 124, and passim).

While the prairies had savage elements—grizzly bears in the Lewis and Clark history are particularly ferocious (1:288 and passim)—they were also beautiful, rich, and fertile. They abounded with game and fruit and appeared almost cultivated. Not in every reference to a prairie do these qualities manifest themselves, but a positive description of the prairies is dominant in the explorers' history.

Washington Irving toured the prairies of Oklahoma on horseback for one month in the fall of 1832, the same year that William Cullen Bryant toured the prairies of Illinois. Irving recorded his impressions of his entire four-month journey in the West in ten notebooks, five of which are extant. The five existing notebooks cover these stages: Cincinnati to St. Louis (September 3–14); Independence, Missouri, to Cabin Creek, seventy miles north of Fort Gibson, Oklahoma (September 26–October 6); Cabin Creek to a point on the Cimarron River (October 6–17); a point on the Little River to Fort Gibson (October 31–November 10); and Fort Gibson to Stack Island, on the Mississippi River (November 11–17). Appealing to a public interest in the prairies, *A Tour on the Prairies*, first published in 1835, covers Irving's journey from October 6 to November 10, when he rode horseback over the prairies of what is now northeastern Oklahoma (see map, frontispiece).

John Francis McDermott characterizes Irving's journey not as exploration but as a "voyage of discovery made by a man who had been long absent from his home."[8] Irving himself announces the patriotic motives of his western tour. Having been abroad for seventeen years, Irving suffered charges of a lack of patriotism and national pride. His return home is, in a sense, a vindication, and his journey west could be seen as a publicity move. He humbly acknowledges his national pride in the "Author's Introduction" to *A*

*Tour on the Prairies:* "I make no boast of my patriotism; I can only say, that, as far as it goes, it is no blind attachment. . . . [I] feel that, after all my ramblings about the world, I can be happiest at home" (8). Irving associates his tour, and therefore the prairies, with American patriotism and nationalism, including ideals of democracy and freedom, which become essential to the prairie metaphor as it develops in the nineteenth century. As Peter Antelyes suggests, Washington's western works "enacted the enterprise of 'making it' in an expanding America."[9]

This passage may be only publicity, not sincerity. Wayne Kime convincingly argues, for example, that A *Tour on the Prairies* was linked from its inception with the earning of money to renovate Irving's home, The Roost, and was "undertaken to satisfy the public's wish for a book about the West by 'Geoffrey Crayon.'"[10] But even if he is writing publicity, or particularly *because* he is writing publicity, Irving associates nationalistic themes with the prairies. Such associations indicate the prairies' popularity and symbolic significance—all the more so if he draws on their popularity to vindicate himself publicly. The immediate success of A *Tour on the Prairies* attests to its popularity and to its help in Irving's quelling the charges of a lack of patriotism and national pride.[11]

Irving's tour of the prairies is more than a patriotic act, however; it is also an emblem of the American experience of discovery. The word *discovery,* which McDermott uses to describe Irving's tour, certainly echoes an essential American theme that comes to include, not only the physical inspection of a previously unknown land (unknown to European emigrants at any rate), but self-introspection. The humble voice in the passage cited immediately above reveals what Irving has discovered during the journey— home and a sense of belonging. The ending of Irving's "Author's Introduction" summarizes more themes associated with American "discovery." Because the tour is in part a "gratification of . . . curiosity," the prairies satisfy the basic human craving for knowledge (8). Because the tour is of a "region fruitful of wonders and adventures," the prairies represent the abundance of an Edenic garden, they imply awe and mystery, and they satisfy the human craving for adventure. Because the tour is a journey "into the wilderness," the prairies become associated with the Puritans' settlement of America.[12] Finally, because *A Tour on the Prairies* is a "simple narrative of everyday occurrences; such as happen to every one who travels the prairies," they represent, indeed unite, common men (9). That is, they produce the democratic man.[13] Irving's thematic associations are the core of the prairie metaphor: the prairies become representative of the American experience from discovery and exploration to settlement.

Apart from the "Author's Introduction," symbolic elements surface throughout the *Tour* itself. Recurring references to the wild game on the prairies, for example, suggest abundance to reiterate the Edenic vision. The landscape teems with elk, bear, turkey, deer, and particularly buffalo. Game is so plentiful, in fact, that rather than carry meat with them, the travelers leave behind what is left from a day's hunting as they break camp (169–70).[14] Commenting on the honeybee, which "swarms in myriads," Irving explicitly relates the prairies' abundance with the Promised Land and paradise: "It seems to me as if these beautiful regions answer literally to the description of the land of promise, 'a land flowing with milk and honey'; for the rich pasturage of the prairies is calculated to sustain herds of cattle as countless as the sands upon the sea-shore, while the flowers with which they are enamelled render them a very paradise for the nectar-seeking bee" (51). Furthermore, as if created for man's benefit, the prairies look like "ornamental cultivation, instead of native wilderness" (36).

Besides reflecting paradise and the Promised Land, the prairies mirror other optimistic and democratic themes and images. Freedom is a main connotation of the prairies' openness. After the party with which Irving is traveling captures a wild horse, Irving is dismayed because the horse loses the "unbounded freedom of the prairie" (150). Later, he is relieved at the escape of a wild mare, who can "remain a free rover of the prairies" (155). Man is likewise free on the prairies. A young Osage guide decides to leave the group and escort one of its members, a young count, on a separate "expedition into the wilderness" (34). When the count and the Indian separate from the main group, Irving comments:

> Such is the glorious independence of man in a savage state. [The Indian] . . . was ready at a moment's warning to rove the world; he carried all his worldly effects with him, and in the absence of artificial wants, possessed the great secret of personal freedom. We of society are slaves, not so much to others as to ourselves; our superfluities are the chains that bind us, impeding every movement of our bodies and thwarting every impulse of our souls. (34)

Irving continues: "Such, at least, were my speculations at the time, though I am not sure but that they took their tone from the enthusiasm of the young Count, who seemed more enchanted than ever with the wild chivalry of the prairies" (34).

Even though Irving qualifies his statement about the relationship between personal freedom and society, he explicitly relates the ideal of freedom to the prairies. At the same time, he broaches another subject that he connects with the prairies—the imagination. He sees at least the possibility that his own imagination is affected by the romantic imagination of the young count. When first introducing the count, Irving also thinks of the capacity of the prairies to stir the imagination. The count is enthusiastic about buffalo hunting: "Indeed the imagination of the young Count had become completely excited on the subject. The grand scenery and wild habits of the prairie had set his spirits madding, and the stories that little Tonish [a half-breed guide] told him of the Indian braves and Indian beauties, of hunting buffaloes and catching wild horses, had set him all agog for a dash into savage life" (15). When Irving admits that he might have been affected by the enthusiastic tone of the count, he comments on the power of the prairie to quicken one's imagination. Like the count's "imagination," Irving's has also been stirred by the "grand scenery and wild habits of the prairie."

The prairies are not entirely affable, however. They pose many hardships and conceal many dangers. The plan to start the tour in wagons, for instance, has to be abandoned when it becomes necessary for the group to cut its way through thickets at the very start (19). Discarding the wagons means not only that they have to ride less comfortably on horseback but also that they cannot bring all the provisions they had planned to. Moreover, the tall grasses hide "sink-holes," "funnel-shaped pits" formed by the "settling of waters after heavy rains," that threaten injury by causing men and horses to stumble into them (159). The fear and the reality of being lost on the expanses of the prairies also come to Irving's mind frequently. The whole group loses the trail once; Old Ryan, a member of the group, gets lost; the count gets lost; and Irving himself gets separated for a night from the group (31, 138, 180–86, 180–81).

The most prominent danger, and the most persistent, is the threat of Indian attacks. Though Irving never encounters hostile Indians, he is always aware of the danger. His opening description of the prairies mostly consists of a discussion of the Indians, who, he says, use the prairies as a war ground: "Mouldering skulls and skeletons, bleaching in some dark ravine, or near the traces of a hunting camp, occasionally mark the scene of a foregone act of blood, and let the wanderer know the dangerous nature of the region he is traversing" (11). Because the Pawnees are nomadic, Irving fears them the most. In one place one day and in another the next, they pose a constant threat, no one knowing where they are at any given time. The Pawnees also have a special talent for hiding in the tall grass, the half-breed guide Tonish tells Irving (94). When the count gets lost, Irving's fear is that the Pawnees have captured him (185).

The dual nature of the prairies is stressed on every level of the book. As I have indicated, in some lengthy passages Irving is entirely positive, in others entirely negative. Some images, like the storms and the openness, reflect both attitudes simultaneously. The storms on the prairies are frightening, but they are also beautiful (101–5). Though the open expanses connote freedom, they also make one feel intensely lonely and vulnerable (152, 175–76).

Irving's use of ocean imagery, an imagery often associated

with the prairies, demonstrates his rendering of the prairies' ambiguity. He first employs a simile, writing that a "clump of trees" on the "undulating" landscape looks from a distance "like a ship at sea" (106). Immediately after, he asserts that the "landscape [derives] sublimity from its vastness and simplicity" (106). Furthermore, equipped properly, an Indian hunter "is like a cruiser on the ocean, perfectly independent of the world, and competent to self-protection and self-maintenance" (28). At another time, however, seeing a Pawnee on a hill is "like descrying a sail at sea in time of war, when it may be either a privateer or a pirate" (84).

Irving's travel book characterizes that genre's treatment of the prairies, though his is more artistically controlled than most others. He makes the essential connections between exploring the prairies and discovering and exploring America. Though he captures the dual nature of the prairies, his general tone remains laudatory. He sounds the themes of freedom and democracy and uses images that recur in poetry about the prairies.

In addition to identifying the ideology that informs the prairie metaphor, these examples of early responses to the prairies and plains exemplify important phenomena related to symbolic makings: they demonstrate the melding of two different ways of seeing (or confronting) the landscape—physical geography and perceptual geography. Frederick Jackson Turner's famous historical essay about the end of the American frontier, "The Significance of the Frontier in American History" (1893), is grounded in physical geography. He asserts that the geography of the western American frontier helped to define the character of the United States and its people—that "the existence of an area of free land, its continuous recession, and the advance of American settlement westward, explain American development." He establishes six frontier lines that border different geographical areas of the United States: "the 'fall line'" of the Atlantic seaboard; "the Allegheny Mountains; the Mississippi; the Missouri where its direction approximates north and south; the line of the arid lands, approximately the ninety-ninth meridian; and the Rocky Mountains."[15] Because of the differences in terrain and the new distances separating the moving pioneers from the older social order, according to Turner, each new area required that the pioneers begin over again.

Perceptual geography takes the opposite position. As James Wreford Watson puts it rather stridently, "Geography is made . . . largely in terms of the country we *perceive,* or are *conditioned* to perceive: *the country of the mind.*"[16] Yi-Fu Tuan begins a discussion of perception and geography with a similar assertion in *Topophilia* (though he later modifies this position, as I will explain): "the ways in which people perceive and evaluate [the earth's] surface are far more varied [than the surface itself]. No two persons see the same reality. No two social groups make precisely the same evaluation of the environment."[17]

These two opposing theories help us understand the complexity and ambiguity of the poetical metaphor of the prairie in the nineteenth-century United States. Turner's perspective is valuable because it is closer to the nineteenth-century mind and reflects a partial truth about how people respond to the prairie. Tuan's perspective is valuable because it more accurately sketches the psychological complexity of the timeless relationship between person and place. In *Topophilia* he sketches the psychological dynamic between person and place, the reciprocity between physical and perceptual geography. Because of "the bewildering wealth of viewpoints [about geography] on both individual and group levels," he writes, "we risk losing sight of the fact that however diverse our perceptions of environment, as members of the same species we are constrained to see things a certain way."[18] He admits, in other words, to the interaction between the ideal and physical geography—a common group of people perceiving something similarly implies an objective complement. He suggests, therefore, that the physical geography affects the people *and* that people's imaginations affect their perception of the geography. Similarly, the collective perception of the prairie landscape by nineteenth-century American poets contained both theoretical perspectives: on one hand, an image of the prairie was constructed by poets according to their ideal conceptions of America; on the other hand, the actual hardships caused by the prairie landscape helped to shape a poetic image.

The metaphor of the prairies and plains in nineteenth-century poetry works, in summary, like this. Like Lewis and Clark's *History*, like Irving's *Tour*, the metaphor is defined by a physical, geographical landscape, one dominant characteristic of which is space—openness. Openness can be variously perceived, and these perceptions, projected onto the prairies and plains, redefine or re-shape their metaphorical geography, as the example of Irving's *Tour* demonstrates. The prairie's openness, along with other characteristics such as flora and fauna, also often suggests that the prairie *is* America—a metaphor of the country's cultural, political, and ideological vastness. Often, therefore, when presented in a poem, a prairie image calls up, in Richard Slotkin's terms, a "large swath of history" and "the dominant ideology."[19]

This introduction only begins to describe the ideology that informs the prairie metaphor and the cultural dynamic that allows the promulgation of the metaphor, and it suggests an ambiguity, in the example of Irving, that is also part of the metaphor. What allows the metaphor, and at times an individual image associated with the prairie, such inclusiveness is the landscape's openness. Openness connotes physical and metaphysical possibility and destiny, as well as impossibility and uncertainty. Openness includes a confirmation of democratic patriotism (equality and freedom) and moral integrity (justice and righteousness), while at the same time it allows the denial of what might be seen as a superficial political morality. Openness includes both sides of manifest destiny: the notions of opportunity and progress as well as their morally reprehensible accompaniments—greed, exploitation, genocide. The metaphor suggests, therefore, a complex point of view, as the prairies and plains reflect the United States' own ambivalence toward itself, its goals, and its ideals.

Using the prairies and plains metaphorically, poets writing in the nineteenth-century United States began to do what Robert Frost suggests is the final step in becoming united with place, in becoming "possessed" by the land: they began to story "the land vaguely realizing westward," enhancing it and making it artful with symbolic images of the prairies.

# CHAPTER TWO

# BREAKING THE SOD
## The Illinois Prairies and the Public Voice of William Cullen Bryant

### BRYANT ON THE ILLINOIS PRAIRIES

While visiting his two brothers, John and Arthur, in Jacksonville, Illinois, during May and June 1832, Bryant recorded his responses to the landscape and its settlers in letters to his wife, Frances, and to his mother. His first few letters tell what route he followed from New York to Jacksonville, commenting on the sights, the conditions of travel, and the traits of the land and people. Bryant describes the ugliness as well as the beauty, and he does not let the details (of what he eats, for example) escape his pen. His route took him alternately by stagecoach, train, and boat through Philadelphia; Hagerstown, Maryland (about eighty miles west of Baltimore); over the Alleghenies; and through Wheeling, Cincinnati, and St. Louis.

Bryant first mentions the prairies in fearful anticipation on June 4, when he is still sixty miles below St. Louis on the Mississippi River. Though commenting on the beauty of the Mississippi Valley, he emphasizes the Black Hawk War, which is threatening enough to make him reject his plan of returning to New York by way of Chicago. Black Hawk, a Sauk Indian, led a group of about one thousand Sauk, Fox, and Kickapoo Indians east across the Mississippi and up the Rock River in violation of an earlier treaty. The resulting "war," which lasted less than three months, between this group of Indians and the state of Illinois aided by federal troops ended with the death of a few white settlers and many Indians.[1]

While Bryant notes that the story of an earlier battle exaggerated the number of dead whites ("the first story was that 52 were lost—then 27—but the truth is said to be 15"), he still asserts that the whites were "defeated."[2] The next day Bryant continues to equate the Indians with savagery and a threatening wilderness. He associates the Black Hawk War with the wilds of Illinois, writing that the bodies of the whites killed in the war "were left to be devoured by hogs and dogs," and then generalizing, "A man has been killed in Buffalo Grove near Galena and it is supposed that an Indian Agent has been murdered by savages. I set out for Jacksonville tomorrow June 6" (1:340). Though Bryant is obviously writing hurriedly, the abrupt tone and staccato sentences give a clue to his thoughts about the threats to life on the prairies and about the need to defend one's self against the hostile Indians.

Bryant also discovers barbarity in the whites. He summarizes a day-long riot in St. Louis in which the citizens, "among whom were some of the most respectable inhabitants of the place," with the "magistrates . . . looking on," tore down two brothels, burned a third, burned the furniture of the fourteen others, and tarred and feathered a black brothel owner—all because a part-Indian prostitute in one brothel stabbed and killed a white man (1:339). The best citizens are in Bryant's eyes racist, vengeful vigilantes, the authorities no better.

Bryant's emphasis on these incidents suggests that he is preparing himself mentally for an excursion into an almost barbaric world. Yet in spite of such uncivilized behavior, St. Louis is not even the wilderness. Bryant eats strawberries at the Prairie House (three or four miles outside St. Louis), but the "old prairie" from which they are gathered looks to him "like any old common field unenclosed and grazed by cows throughout the year" (1:340). So Bryant's first glimpse of the prairie is anticlimactic. It is already disappearing, becoming civilized as the wilderness is tamed and put to use. (The theme of a disappearing wilderness he will use later in his prairie poems.) His reference to "any old common field" contradicts the savagery he earlier associated with the prairie, and his ambivalence begins to surface.

In his June 12 letter to Frances, Bryant records his first responses to the actual, wild prairie. He is on the Illinois River:

> We stopped to take in wood on the west shore and I proceeded a few rods through the forest to take my first look at a natural prairie. It was one of the wet or alluvial prairies. The soil was black and rather moist and soft, and as level as if the surface had been adjusted by some instrument of art. To the north and south along the river it stretched to an extent of which I cannot judge, but to the east it was bounded at the distance of about five miles by a chain of rounded eminences, their sides principally covered with grass and their summits with wood forming the commencement of the uplands on which the dry prairies are situated. The prairie itself was covered with coarse rank grass four or five feet in height intermingled with a few flowers. Here and there stood a tu[lip tree?] in the midst of the wilderness of verdure. (1:342, brackets are the editors' of the *Letters*)

Bryant's language here is important. While his tone is at first one of an objective observer as he describes the soil and nature of the prairie, his gradual tonal shift suggests that the prairie, as he sees it for the first time, immediately takes on a figurative significance. First, the prairie's flatness requires a simile to describe it, and it is important that the comparison includes an "instrument of art." The second quality to strike him is the "extent" of the prairie. Bounded by a "chain of rounded eminences" about five miles from the river, it is unbounded to the north and south as far as the eye can see. Bryant does, necessarily, assume northern and southern boundaries, but these borders are in his mind. Paradoxically, then, the prairie metaphorically reconciles boundaries and limitlessness, since the prairie is simultaneously bounded and unbounded. Such invention indicates the most significant quality of the prairie—an openness that allows the poet to set his own imaginative limits.

After briefly returning to the voice of the objective observer, Bryant ends this first description of the prairie with the quintessential American metaphor. Because "wilderness of verdure" reflects an image that at Bryant's time was already an American literary convention, it is not unusual that this image would come to mind. What is unique is the geography to which it is applied, and which Bryant begins to shape imaginatively into a "perceptual geography."

Bryant's first reaction to Jacksonville and its surrounding prairie continues to demonstrate his ambivalence. At first he is as cruelly objective as in his earlier description of the riot in St. Louis, calling Jacksonville

> a horribly ugly little village composed of little shops and dwellings stuck close together around a dirty square in the middle of which stands the ugliest of possible brick court houses with a spire and weathercock on its top. The surrounding country is a bare green plain, with gentle undulations of surface unenlivened by a single tree, save what you see at a distance on the edge of the prairie in the centre of which the village stands. (1:343)

Yet this "unenlivened plain" has "gentle undulations" and, as the continuation of the passage quoted here reveals, it is rich in growth, "rank" (itself a curiously ambiguous word suggesting both fecundity and odors of decay). It is, furthermore, "partly enclosed" and "partly open." To heighten the paradox, Bryant refers to "gaudy flowers," thus reversing his original idea of ugliness. ("Gaudy" itself is ambiguous.) In yet another quick reversal he shows that he is *imagining* the flowers, as he lets Frances know that the beauty of them is not now present. Time also shifts quickly. First, he mentions the "gaudy flowers" as if they were present, but quickly adds, "this is not however the flowering season." They were in bloom a "fortnight since." Then he suddenly projects to the future, when the fields "will soon be yellow with other syngenesious plants." Responding ambivalently, then, to an open landscape, Bryant records the resulting contrasts and contradictions.

To the voices of the objective observer and the imaginatively responding poet is added the voice of the jokester, which first enters after Bryant, the observer, describes the spartan log cabin on his brother Arthur's farm. Since houses are small on the prairies, many consisting of only one room, Bryant notes, "No room here is furnished unless it has a bed" (1:343). Aware of the humor that could derive from this condition, he writes facetiously to Frances: "Shall I confess the truth to you, and suffer you to judge whether I am not what the French call *un homme à bonnes fortunes?* Have I not slept in the same apartment with two young ladies? And am I not . . . to sleep this night in the same room with another, an accomplished young lady . . . whose native language is French . . . ?" (1:343)

Earlier Bryant was the moralist when he witnessed an incident in which a "set of boors" occupied a covered wagon and "obliged" a woman "carrying an infant" to ride in an uncovered one. His judgment was curt: "a bad specimen of the manners of the people here." (1:342). Though he does admit he never saw any further "incivility to ladies," we must assume because of his judgment that he witnessed social improprieties comparable to this one. Now, however, he is more understanding of the changes that the frontier works on society and its standards. As he creates his geography of the mind, at the same time the physical geography works changes on him.

The actual account of the five-day horseback journey that William and John took on the prairies is recorded in a lengthy letter to Frances dated June 19, 1832, two days after the completion of the tour. The trip began in Jacksonville on June 13 (see map, frontispiece). On the first day they rode east to Springfield. On the second day they turned north and spent the night in a cabin north of Sugar Creek. Day three brought them to Pleasant Grove, about eight miles from Pekin. The return to Jacksonville took the last two days. On the last evening, June 16, they stopped at a prairie cabin belonging to an older couple.

While Bryant's tone in this letter echoes some of the disgust that he feels for the places and people he had earlier encountered, it also catches the humor. And though he does not idealize his vision of the prairie as he does in his poems, neither does he, as some critics have suggested, completely scorn it. He is, rather, throughout the letters, the objective observer—the practical visitor helping his brother decide on a suitable location for settling. Bryant is himself sufficiently impressed with the country to consider buying some land as an investment. The informing impulse of the June 19 letter, however, remains ambivalent, as Bryant weighs his responses to the frontier.

Before he begins his journey, he displays his ambivalence. He writes on June 13 (in a letter dated June 12) that he will carry only saddlebags and an umbrella, trusting to "Providence" for food. While Bryant may be joking, the puritanical echoes of "Providence" sound throughout this entry, as do Edenic echoes:

> The forests are of a very large growth and contain a greater variety of trees than are common to the eastward. The soil of the open country is fat and fertile and the growth of all the vegetable tribes is rapid and strong to a degree unknown in your country. . . . Wild plums grow in large thickets loaded with a profusion of fruit said to be of excellent flavour. The earth in the woods is covered with May-apples not yet ripe, and in the enclosed prairies with large fine strawberries now in their perfection. Wild gooseberries with smooth fruit are produced in abundance. (1:344)

The perfection of this place is further evident in its gentleness (paradoxical to its earlier-characterized savagery): "There is not a stone or pebble or bit of gravel in all these prairies. A plough lasts a man his life time, a hoe never wears out and the horses go unshod" (1:344). Along with the sense of paradox, Bryant's ambivalence exposes itself within these Edenic allusions. While noting that the Illinois prairie "is salubrious and . . . the most fertile country I ever saw," he also shies away from such perfection, perhaps instinctively mistrusting such easy traditional, metaphoric constructs: he comments, "at the same time I do not think it beautiful" (1:344).

In the June 19 letter Bryant has little to say of the first day. He dismisses the town because it strikes him very unfavorably: "the houses are not so good, a considerable proportion of them being miserable log cabins, and the whole town having an appearance of dirt and discomfort" (1:345). After spending the night in a filthy tavern, he and John head north.

The second day covers a variety of country and experience, implying the variety and unexpectedness that become part of the metaphor of the prairie in his poetry. He notes "large tracts covered with hazel bushes among which grew the red lily and the *painted cup*, a large scarlet flower" (1:345, Bryant's emphasis). Aside from this appositional phrase, he offers no description of the scene nor flower—a telling absence, since Bryant chose to write a poem about this flower ten years later, after another trip to Illinois. Similarly, Bryant gives no details about crossing a "prairie seven or eight miles in width" (1:345). In fact, the only panoramic picture of a prairie that he gives in his letters is the one quoted above from his June 12 letter. But the fact remains that time, memory, and imagination are able to work on the initial, and seemingly unimpressive, sighting of the flower and the expansive prairie. In this sense the absent description of the prairies acknowledges a special poetic quality. Significantly, absence connotes an openness that can be variously interpreted.

This lack of physical description of the land sets the precedent for the rest of the letter. In fact, Bryant will not consciously describe the land itself until he leaves Jacksonville. He mentions prairies, however expansive, only in connection with another topic, which asserts itself as more important. Indeed, the longest description of the landscape crossed on horseback is of a pasture near the cabin at which they spent the night, a pasture that is no longer wild, natural prairie, but is "a little spot of ground enclosed from the prairie and which appeared when we saw it the next morning to be closely grazed to the very roots of the herbage"

(1:346). The most detailed description is of a degenerating prairie, a theme that Bryant is aware of, and that will appear in "The Prairies." Bryant's responses are rather to the cabins, people, streams, meals, and incidents that one encounters when traveling on the prairies. The prairies themselves seem to be reserved for later poetic expression.[3]

The first incident of importance on the second day is the fording of the Sangamon, which causes no problem but is nonetheless significant in that rivers and streams form an important part of the prairie's physical and metaphorical landscape. They often have an ambiguous and paradoxical character, as Bryant suggests in this letter. The Sangamon is both muddy and clear: because its bottom is "solid rock," it "rolled its transparent waters," but "the immediate edge of the river was muddy" (1:345). The Sangamon also provides some contour to the prairie. Likewise, water in the prairie metaphor often suggests boundaries and helps define the prairies physically. The pair also ford Salt Creek, a "beautiful stream perfectly clear and flowing over pebbles and gravel" (1:346). Though John and William successfully ford Salt Creek, a man traveling with another party is thrown into the water as the result of crossing in a place that became so deep that his companions had to swim their horses. Seemingly innocuous streams conceal threats in their clear yet impenetrable waters and unsuspected depths.

An important incident occurs this day while William and John are eating wild strawberries. William's horse starts, throws his gear, and gallops back toward Springfield. Thinking his trip is over, Bryant starts walking toward Springfield, too, but in about two miles he meets a man riding his escaped horse, and the animal is unexpectedly recovered. Bryant does not exclaim about the miraculous recovery of the horse: perhaps Providence is credited with the animal's return. He merely adds that "he was very glad to discover" that the man had his horse, and he humorously ends the episode with the understatement "I then went back to the strawberries and finished them" (1:346). It is as if such an outstanding coincidence of losing and recovering a horse in this great expanse is not out of the ordinary at all, but is almost expected.

This second reference to strawberries stresses the importance of food, which becomes a frequent topic in Bryant's letters from Illinois. Usually food is obtained at a settler's home. Bryant often catalogs the food he is served as a way of characterizing the persons and places he visits. His meals on the prairie become especially important, therefore, because they differ so drastically from what he is used to. Like the prairie itself, at times the meals are wholesome and tasty, though basic and simple. Other times they are repulsive. The food, like the prairie, reflects the paradoxical nature of the people and the place, but one must accept what is given. The midday meal this second day of the journey, for instance, consists of "a rasher of bacon, a radish, bread and milk" (1:345).

That evening John and William stop at a cabin to spend the night—private cabins being the inns of the prairies. As always, Bryant describes the cabin, but this one is particularly revolting. Unlike the cabin of the people who fed them their afternoon meal—which had the luxury of two rooms "and in one of them only one bed," which offered them a "comfortable" way to live, and was no mere cabin but a "house" (1:346)—the cabin this evening is a

> dwelling . . . of the most wretched description. It consisted of but one room about half of which was taken up with beds and cribs, on one of which lay a man sick with fever, and on another sprawled two or three children besides several who were asleep on the floor and all of whom were brown with dirt. In an enormous fireplace blazed a huge fire built against an enormous backlog reduced to a glowing coal, and before it the hostess and her daughter were busy in cooking a supper for several travellers who were sitting under a kind of piazza in front of the house or standing in the yard. As it was a great deal too hot in the house and a little too cool and damp in the night air we endeavoured to make the balance even by warming ourselves in the house and cooling ourselves out of doors alternately. (1:346)

The meal is as repulsive as the conditions and the people: "About ten o'clock the sweaty hostess gave us our supper consisting of warm cakes, bacon coffee [perhaps the missing comma is intentional] and lettuce with bacon grease poured over it" (1:346). As a climax to this disagreeable evening, Bryant must sleep on the floor of the cabin, which is crowded with other travelers. But the truly repulsive detail is "the small passage left [amid the sleepers] for the sick man to get to the door" (1:347). John and William leave early the next morning after a sleepless night.

The account of the third and fourth days reiterates by now common topics and techniques. The large prairie crossed on the third day is not described in any detail: "We crossed the fifteen mile prairie and nearly three miles beyond came to the Mackinaw a fine clear stream . . . which we forded, and about a half a mile beyond came to a house where live a Quaker family of the name of Wilson. Here we got a nice breakfast" (1:347). This passage condenses the prairie experience so far—referring not to the prairie but to a stream, house, people, food. The movement, literal and figurative, is, as the diction suggests, always *beyond* the prairie.

Because of fatigue, hot weather, and lazy and obstinate horses, John and William decide to return to Jacksonville the next day. This fourth day of the journey, June 16, they "crossed the large prairie already mentioned by a newer and more direct road to Jacksonville." Bryant continues to ignore the prairie itself in his description. They pass two houses, one at "the edge of a small wood on an eminence in the midst of the prairie" (1:347). The other, contradictorily, stands empty because of "sickness and want of water" (1:348). The brothers spend this night in a comfortable house, in which they eat, at their own request, only bread and milk. The voice of the humorist also returns. The Dutch woman of this house, on hearing Bryant say that he was a Yankee who had "lived among the Dutch in New York," "remarked that she reckoned that was the reason I did not talk like a Yankee. I replied that no doubt living among the Dutch had improved my English" (1:348). In better spirits, because returning to Jacksonville, Bryant is kinder to the prairie and lighthearted toward its people.

The final day of the horseback tour is uneventful but significant because Bryant summarizes his attitude toward the prairie and his experiences on it. A brief entry sets the squalid against the clean but stark. Of the first *cabin* he writes:

> In looking for a place to feed our horses I asked for corn at the cabin of an old settler named Wilson where I saw a fat dusky looking woman barefoot with six children as dirty as pigs and shaggy as bears. She was lousing one of them and cracking the unfortunate insects between her thumbnails. I was very glad when she told me that she had no corn nor oats. (1:348)

Contrarily, of the next *house* he writes:

> At the next house we found corn and seeing a little boy of two years old running about with a clean face I told John that we should get a clean breakfast. I was right. The man whose name was Short had a tall young wife in a clean cotton gown and shoes and stockings. She baked us some cakes fried some bacon and made a cup of coffee which being put on a clean table cloth and recommended by a good appetite was swallowed with some eagerness. (1:348)

Bryant's ambivalent response to the prairies comes through clearly. The "cabin" opposes the "house"; the filth, the cleanliness; the bare feet, the shoes and stockings; the lack of nourishment, the good quality of food and eager appetite; the seriousness, the humor with the name of Short; the vulgarity of crushing the lice, the nourishing act of cooking. Bryant relies here on his three dominant images for revealing the characters of the people and place—the dwelling, the food, and the people themselves.

Bryant ends his June 19 entry to Frances with disparaging comments on his trip as a whole: "About nine in the evening we reached Wiswall's very glad to repose from a journey which had been performed in exceedingly hot weather, on horses which required constant flogging to keep them awake, and in which we had not slept at the rate of more than three hours a night." The next day he feels isolated and trapped, writing curtly, "I have seen every thing which this place has to show me and am ready to set out this moment if I had any way of getting on" (1:349).

This lengthy letter to Frances is important as Bryant's first extended impression of the prairie. His initial responses are replete with paradoxes, which manifest themselves, for example, in his characterization of the people on the Illinois prairies. Some prepare food that is basic and wholesome; others eat food that is repulsive and vile. Some live in dilapidated cabins; others live in cozy houses. Some are ignorant drinkers and brawlers; others are intelligent and moral. The tones Bryant uses to portray these people are also varied. He is objective observer, moralist, humorist, judgmental deprecator, and advocate for the prairies and settlers.

Though his first impressions of the prairie are hardly complimentary, his letters from the Illinois prairie refer to things and ideas that later play an important part in his poetry of the prairie—solitude, beauty, Indian mounds, disappearing wilderness, and an encroaching and destructive civilization. Significantly, negative images and ideas of filth, exhaustion, isolation, danger, and savagery are emphasized in the letter but later almost ignored in the poems. The panoramic views of the prairies themselves are conspicuously absent from his letters. But then, openness is not to be objectively described, or if described, is done so figuratively through the dwellings, nourishment, people, and thoughts that it informs and that inform it. Bryant's ambivalence has become the prairie's paradoxical or ambiguous nature, and its one clear characteristic.

## BRYANT'S RETURN TO NEW YORK

Bryant's changing view of the prairies becomes evident in the letters about the prairies that he writes after distancing himself, both in time and place, from Illinois and after musing over his impressions. The landscape begins to become metaphor. Letters to his wife, his mother, and Richard Henry Dana show the steps through which he idealizes the prairies until he finally publishes "The Prairies."

His letter to Frances dated June 28, 29, and 30 shows this next step of his poetic process. He begins by associating Jacksonville and hell: "I was detained in Jacksonville four or five days, waiting for a conveyance to take me to the Illinois river, for Jacksonville like another place we read of though very easy to get into is hard to get out of" (1:350). The statement, though hardly complimentary, is slightly tempered by his immediate shift to an objective tone when he describes the specific means of conveyance in and out of town.

Bryant's tone continues to fluctuate. Not despising the place entirely, he complains, rather, of a stasis while he had to wait before leaving Jacksonville: "The only incident which signalized the time . . . was the death of a turkey buzzard" (1:351). This seems an appropriate image of the place, as does the dead hog whose "odour gave notice" to the buzzards. But after these derogatory statements, Bryant's letter assumes the tone of an ornithology book. A young man shoots the buzzard so Bryant can inspect it, and Bryant writes objectively: "It is a kind of vulture much resembling those figured in books of natural history with a bald wrinkled head and curving bill. The size is apparently equal to that of a middle sized turkey and the plumage is nearly the colour of the darker coloured turkeys. The body is however small and light in proportion to its apparent size, but the wings are very long" (1:351). He shows his interest in the things of the place, suggesting that he mentally retains a running catalog of the sights and experiences. He notes the vulture's disgusting method of defense: "to eject from its stomach upon its enemy the offensive food it has swallowed." This bird, however, also has positive qualities: it rids the country of carrion, and significantly, Bryant adds, "The quills are sometimes used for writing" (1:351).

After these tonal shifts, he writes of the Illinois wildlife in words that echo the myths of Eden and New Canaan:

Illinois abounds in game. The plover the killdeer or sand-piper and marsh quail abound in the prairies, and the common quail in the grounds where there are thickets, or scattered trees. The woods abound with squirrels rabbits pigeons, mourning doves, and the autumn brings the prairie hens and wild turkeys in flocks about the wheat stacks. There is a bird esteemed a great delicacy here called the wood cock, a different bird from that known by the name in New York markets. It is a large black bird of the wood pecker species. (1:351)

"Abound" appears three times in the first three sentences. The catalog itself suggests abundance and provision. The turkeys appear in "flocks," and the wood cock is "esteemed." Clearly Bryant's point of view has changed from his June 19 reference to wolves (which he did not see) and the "green headed prairie fly" that plagued him and John while on horseback. This list of animals is, in fact, the longest in all his letters about the prairies.

Even his attitude toward Jacksonville has been assuaged. He recalls that on June 23 he was "obliged to stay in that hot dirty place" and that a fight among drunks broke out, but unlike the earlier riot in St. Louis (nearer to civilization), this time a "peace officer" stops the fight. He ends with a comment about his brother Cyrus, who is at that time on his way to Illinois, but from whom Bryant has not yet heard. "I hope the Indians have not got him" (1:351), he writes, implying the threat of the savages emphasized before William's arrival in Jacksonville. That threat, however, has now lost its power, as suggested by the casual way the sentence is interjected, for immediately after it, Bryant turns to the mundane matter of his travel schedule.

The most telling comments, however, appear in the last half of his June 28 entry. Viewing the Western shore of the Mississippi en route to St. Louis, he romanticizes: "Sometimes the rocks flamed with wild roses, for here and in Illinois grows a rose the gayest and most profuse of flowers of any of its tribe. The flowers just opened are of a deep crimson, those which are more unfolded are of all shades between this and a pale damask. I have provided myself with some of the seeds" (1:352). The flower must be the rose, conventionally the ideal flower. In Illinois, of course, it must necessarily be wild.

As the beauty of the Illinois landscape presses into his mind, Bryant seems to forget the discomforts of his arduous journey. Instead of wishing for nothing else than quickly to be home with his family, he admits to a "vague desire to wander further"—not only south, but northwest, where the "Missouri stretch[es] eighteen hundred miles into the uninhabited interior" (1:352). Perhaps it is the idea of an "uninhabited interior" that attracts him, a still-pristine landscape that is as yet untouched by the destructive powers of civilization.

Regardless, Bryant writes to Frances that she "will not be surprised" by his sense of wanderlust; but after reading her husband's previous letters, Frances would have had enough evidence of the discomfort of travel in the West to be surprised indeed. Since Bryant's conception of the prairie is already shifting while his poetic imagination works, however, he assumes that Frances would understand his "vague desire." She in fact might have, but Bryant is nonetheless erasing from his mind some of what he had written earlier on paper.

Some negative comments about the West are interjected into the last half of the letter: he is disgusted with the dirt, with the "western man's notion [that] living well is to have plenty of meat" (1:352). (Bryant's vegetarian tendencies have perhaps been offended.) He considers the "common brush which in every western steamboat hangs by one of the looking glasses" an "enormity of nastiness" (1:353). He ends his June 28 entry with a recognition of the hardship a woman would suffer if she visited Illinois. But even these negative statements do not overshadow the penultimate paragraph: "Hitherto my journey as it has been the longest so it has been altogether the most delightful I ever took. Had I those with me whom I have left behind I could imagine nothing more pleasant. Travelling to the west had been associated in my mind with the idea of hard[ship]—it is mere pastime" (1:352; brackets are those of the editors of *Letters*). In only eleven days he has put the very real hardships completely out of mind.

Bryant's letter to his mother about his trip, dated August 23, 1832, further demonstrates how he shapes his material. He begins with information about the poor corn crops in Illinois and the problems Arthur and John have had with their crops. He comments on the hardships the two brothers endure, especially during the winter, because of the poor state of their cabin. He adds disparagingly, if humorously, "and as for privies I do not believe there are a dozen in all Illinois except in the villages" (1:356). He writes later that during their five-day trip on the prairies he and John slept "at night in log cabins where the whole family pigged together in one room" (1:356). Yet Bryant notes that he left John money to purchase 160 acres for him—hardly the action of someone who feels negatively about the prairies. He is taking advantage of the 1820 Public Lands Act, which lowered the minimum land purchase to 80 acres and the minimum price to $1.25 per acre. David J. Baxter published the records of Bryant's land transactions in Illinois to show that "Bryant, . . . in 1837, was an absentee landlord, even though a small one, buying cheaply and selling at a profit to new settlers, or, while land values increased, renting his land to tenant farmers and reinvesting the proceeds."[4] Even though Bryant is investing in cheap government land and not necessarily intending to live on it himself, he certainly recognizes its potential desirability and value.

In this letter he comments further on the positive qualities of the land:

> the country, at least such parts of it as I have seen, is extraordinarily fertile, it is very level however, and some parts of it are destitute of water. I do not believe there is a more productive country on the face of the earth. The soil is a deep rich black, fine mould which when mixed with water makes a composition almost as black as the Extract of Gentian and as sleek looking. It is in short the richest garden soil. I believe the upland prairies to be quite healthy. (1:356–57)

While this passage shows why he might be interested in investing in the land, it also shows, in the diction derived from the Edenic metaphor, the ideal quality he imparts to it. Describing the visual beauty and general character of the land, he is slightly less optimistic, though he remains objective: "The general aspect of the country is monotonous,—it wants clear running streams, and has only the beauty which arises from a gently undulating surface and luxuriance of vegetation" (1:357).

Though he asserts that the people are generally ignorant and "inclined to get drunk and fight on Saturdays," he speaks more kindly of Jacksonville itself. He notes again that it "is one of the ugliest and most unpleasant places I ever saw," but it is now also "a remarkably moral place—more so than most villages in New England, and the people seem intelligent." In fact, he sees the general "population of Illinois improving." He seems to have forgotten some unpleasant experiences when he writes, "I met with nothing but civility and kindness on my journey of a hundred miles in the interior" (1:357). At the end of this letter Bryant depicts a new side of Jacksonville, one not revealed in his letters from Illinois. Because "the people are more intelligent and orderly and the opportunities of education will be better there than in any other part of the state," he writes, "Jacksonville is on some accounts a desirable place to live in" (1:358).

The threat from the Indians seems to have lessened now, too. Now heard from, Cyrus has explained that on his journey to Jacksonville he had had to leave his sick horse and travel on foot. "From Chicago to Iroquois 75 miles he saw no white person. . . . [and he] camped one night among the Pottawattomies" (1:357). On his three-hundred-mile trek from Chicago to Danville to Jacksonville, though Cyrus suffered much thirst and fatigue because of the heavy pack and hot weather, he encountered no problem with Indians.

Bryant could, of course, be tempering this letter to his mother for her sake, yet he has been frank with her about the poor corn crop, the poor living conditions of her sons, the "privies," the drinking, and the fighting. In other letters to her he does not withhold his thoughts about her sons' ventures in the West, no matter how discouraging they may be. Though this letter does not sound as positive as his letter of June 28, 29, and 30 to Frances, the comparison of the two clarifies Bryant's process of revision—his vacillating between actuality and ideality.

One and a half months after writing this letter to his mother, Bryant writes to Richard Henry Dana and says nothing negative of the prairies. He also mentions an idea that becomes very important in "The Prairies"—the possibility of the prairies being cultivated by a race of people existing previously to the Indians. He begins his October 8 letter by describing his trip generally, but he leaves out the disgusting details of the wretched night in the crowded cabin: "I have seen the great west, where I ate corn bread and hominy, & slept in log houses with twenty men women and children in the same room" (1:360). A few sentences later he idealizes:

> At Jacksonville I got on a horse and travelled about a hundred miles to the northward over the immense prairies with scattered settlements on the edges of the groves. These prairies, of a soft fertile garden soil, and a smooth undulating surface, on which you may put a horse to full speed, covered with high thinly growing grass, full of weeds and gaudy flowers, and destitute of bushes or trees, perpetually brought to my mind the idea of their having been once cultivated. They looked to me like the fields of a race which had passed away, whose enclosures and habitations had decayed, but on those vast and rich plains smoothed and levelled by tillage the forest has not yet encroached. (1:360)

The previously absent description of the prairies is now being developed, and the immensity of the prairies allows various metaphorical reverberations. The diction of fertility and fullness suggests the

Edenic metaphor as well as the fertility of poetic creation: the "rank," "high thinly growing grass" and the "gaudy flowers" both find their way into "The Prairies" ("rank" and "gaudy flowers" also appeared in earlier letters from Illinois). The "undulating surface" takes on not only the poetic and fluid nature of the ocean but also the ocean's metaphorical associations with the soul. Finally, the idea of a previous race of people on the prairies eventually suggests the two themes of the earth as a sepulcher and the changing "forms of being," both of which Bryant uses in "The Prairies." The romantic imagination is plainly at work here, for there is no hint in the earlier letters of the idea of previous cultivation being "perpetually brought to . . . mind."[5]

First published in *The Knickerbocker* in December 1833, "The Prairies" was substantially written before November 1833, but not much earlier. In a letter to Dana, November 2, 1833, Bryant first mentions the poem, writing that he is not yet finished because "the conclusion gives me some perplexity" and stating, "I have sometimes kept a poem for weeks before I could do it in a manner with which I was at all pleased" (1:383). This last sentence implies that he has not been working on "The Prairies" very long. Certainly he did not write it, as Parke Godwin claims in his edition of Bryant's *Poetical Works*, while in Illinois or immediately after his visit.[6] If he had been writing it then, he would have no doubt mentioned the poem to Dana in his October 8, 1832, letter.

On November 11, 1833, Bryant writes to Dana again about changes for the 1834 edition of *Poems:*

> The words "that to the gazes seem" in the second line
> of the Prairies strike me as feeble. I wish the commence-
> ment of that poem to stand thus.

> These are the gardens of the desert, these
> The unshorn fields, boundless and beautiful,
> And fresh as the young earth ere man had sinned—
> The Prairies, &c, &c. (*Letters* 1:385)

Besides helping to date the writing of "The Prairies," this letter provides insight into Bryant's creative process: he was revising his view of the prairie right up to his publication deadlines. Indeed, the poem, especially the first few lines, undergoes substantial revision even after the poem is in print.

In his letters written after he leaves Jacksonville, Bryant begins to resolve his ambivalence (though he never does so completely) by imaginatively re-creating the prairies. As his conception of the prairies and of what they signify shifts in his mind, he idealizes his original impressions, then recalls his earlier sights of squalor, then again rejects the filth and moral degeneration of the place and its people. As he considers and reconsiders his emotional and intellectual responses, he records the process of transforming the prairies into something ideal and idyllic, emphasizing their grandeur and nobleness. The physical geography and perceptual geography conjoin, and the prairie becomes a metaphor with constant interaction between its developer and the place. There is a continual shaping and reshaping, sifting and shifting—"airy undulations"—of vision and revision.

## BRYANT'S "POETIC" PRAIRIES

> These are the gardens of the Desert, these
> The unshorn fields, boundless and beautiful,
> For which the speech of England has no name—
> The Prairies.[7]

Thus William Cullen Bryant proclaims the inadequacy of the English language to speak for America. These opening lines of "The Prairies" assert that here is an American poet consciously shaping an American poetic language. While Bryant's derivative English diction—that is, Wordsworthian diction—is cited by critics, his success in initiating an American diction remains virtually unexamined.[8] Some of his poems do begin to shape an American poetic language by establishing, to use D. H. Lawrence's phrase, a "spirit of place." Bryant characterizes this place by painting word pictures and by naming the *things* of the place. In the poems of the prairies, particularly in "The Prairies," he becomes even more assertive. In addition to relying on his technique of a language picture to create a spirit of place, he suggests the need for a new mythology. Though he alludes to the conventional mythology of the New Promised Land, Bryant emphasizes a unique mythos of the New World, and thus he creates an entirely fresh context for his language. Portraying the uniqueness of the new place and its native mythology, Bryant redefines the words that describe them. Rather than carry the weighty connotations of an old, European culture, the words express America's essence.[9]

Bryant's picture-making technique is fully examined by Donald A. Ringe in *The Pictorial Mode: Space and Time in the Art of Bryant, Irving, and Cooper*.[10] Ringe demonstrates that this technique shows Bryant's artistic concern for capturing the American landscape's uniqueness in his poetry. Linking Bryant with the Hudson River school of painting, he suggests that their main efforts were to create an art specific to America. Like the painters of the Hudson River school, Bryant establishes the spirit of place by attention both to the expanse and to the details of nature. This place, this new context, helps reciprocally to define the terms used in the poems. Those terms, particularly the ones that describe the detail, are for Bryant often lists of names.

Albert F. McLean, Jr., claims that Bryant's "return to Nature for diction meant merely the naming of indigenous plants, birds, and animals in the simple vernacular and the brief, infrequent mention of place names in his poems." Setting Bryant against Whitman, Thoreau, Melville, and Twain, McLean claims that Bryant "failed to sense the implications of his theory"—"the downright earthiness of the American vernacular, the latent ironies and humor of dialect, the possibilities of 'organic' expression which united matter and idea in a single word or phrase."[11] "The Prairies," however, antedates the major works, or language experiments, of those other writers, and naming is a necessary beginning for cultivating a new language, as Bryant himself states. He writes at the end of his third lecture on poetry, "On Poetry in Relation to Our Age and Country" (1825), with some vehemence against the charge that

Americans speak a "transplanted" language that they are not likely to wield with much "force, effect, and grace":

> It seems to me that this is one of the most unsubstantial of all the brood of phantoms which have been conjured up to alarm us. . . . the copious and flexible dialect we speak . . . has grown up, as every forcible and beautiful language has done, among a simple and unlettered people; *it has accommodated itself,* in the first place, *to the things of nature, and,* as civilization advanced, *to the things of art;* and thus it has become a language full of picturesque forms of expression. (*Prose* 1:34, my emphasis)

According to Bryant, then, the creation of a new language for a new world begins with the naming of the things of that world, so Bryant's "merely naming," as McLean would have it, need not be *mere* at all, as Adam's task of naming was not, because in naming he captured the essence of the thing named and became master of it.

When he names, Bryant does what Emerson later writes about. For Emerson the poet's task of naming is not a simple one. In "The Poet" Emerson writes: "the poet is the Namer, or Language-maker, naming things sometimes after their appearance, sometimes after their essence, and giving to every one its own name and not another's, thereby rejoicing the intellect. . . . the poet names the thing because he sees it, or comes one step nearer to it than any other" (*Essays* 13). In "Poetry and Imagination" Emerson is even more direct:

> In the ocean, in fire, in the sky, in the forest, [man] finds facts adequate and as large as he. As his thoughts are deeper than he can fathom, so also are these. It is easier to read Sancrit, to decipher the arrow-head character, than to interpret these familiar sights. *It is even much to name them.* Thus Thomson's Seasons and the best parts of many old and many new poets are simply enumerations by a person who felt the beauty of the

common sights and sounds, without any attempt to draw a moral or affix a meaning. (*Letters and Social Aims* 22–23; my emphasis)

Earlier, in "The Prairies" Bryant himself had done in poetry what Emerson developed in his prose statements:

The Prairies. I behold them for the first,
And my heart swells, while the dilated sight
Takes in the encircling vastness. (184)

The name of the place comes first. The namer is also, like Adam, the first man to behold them. For him the prairies encircle all, and their majesty affects the seat of his emotions and the very core of his being. Creating in an Emersonian sense, then, Bryant's naming captures the essence of the new things in the new world confronted for the first time by the first man. What Betsy Erkkila states about Walt Whitman's use of foreign (particularly French) terms can, therefore, also be said of Bryant's language, albeit Bryant's contribution along these lines is less than Whitman's: his language is part of a "national debate about the relationship between language and culture in America."[12]

Granted, Bryant wrote poems with American themes that ask to be rendered in an American diction but that are not. While "The Indian Girl's Lament" (1823) contains the words "mocsen," "wampum-belts," "bison's hide," and "bow and arrows"—things associated with America—the last eight stanzas are supposedly in the girl's "woodland tongue." But no Indian maiden would speak as she does, even in translation. The situation in "An Indian Story" (1824) is similar. Bryant names the hunter-warrior, "Maquon," and two trees, the "larch" and "sassafras." But neither Maquon's words nor the words of the narrator suggest an American diction. Similarly, the only clues to the cultural and racial identity of the speaker of "An Indian at the Burial Place of His Fathers" (1824) are the title and the first-person narration. These and other legendlike poems of native Americans are obvious candidates for an American diction.

But none is written with any serious attempt to create or sustain an American poetic language.

We cannot dismiss Bryant's diction on these examples alone, however, for there are other poems in which he does write with an American diction. Because most of the legend poems cited above were written before "The Prairies" and Bryant's other prairie poems, they are not strong evidence against Bryant's American diction. The legend poems, however, do help to set in relief Bryant's poems that use American words more effectively.

"Robert of Lincoln" (1855) is certainly experimental with its language. The boastful tone characterizes this American songbird as an audacious braggart. It is a tone befitting an American voice that mocks English tradition. The simplicity of diction echoes the bird's chirping and his quickness, further characterizing him and reinforcing the tone. The simple diction also reflects the plainness of the female bird, which represents the American Quaker, and suggests the American "plain style." The refrains, "Spink, spank, spink" and "Chee, chee, chee," are coined words that give voice to this American songbird. Not only does the refrain "Bob-o-link" echo the bird's song, but it also sounds in the American vernacular the name of the bird, shortened ironically from the mocking Anglican title, "Robert of Lincoln."

Like "To Cole, the Painter, Departing for Europe," which shows Bryant's tendency to catalog and thus announces his intentions toward an American diction, two other poems introduce names of western things. "The Maiden's Sorrow" (1842) bemoans the death of a lover in the "distant West," so the flowers named are explicitly associated with the New World and its most recently explored regions. The violets on the grave are not a particularly American image (though they are American, too), but the "crimson phlox and moccasin-flower" are. "The Hunter's Serenade" (1828), also set in the American West, names even more particularly American things: the vast, American "savannas"; "prairie fowl"; "meadows red with blossoms"; and the American "sycamore." The mounds built by the early prairie dwellers, which figure significantly in "The Prairies," are also mentioned in this poem.

The whole of "The Fountain" (1839) is an American catalog. As the poem lists the names of things that have risen, lived, and given way to new things, it condenses the American experience. It begins by naming the plants, particularly trees and wildflowers: "viburnum," "maple," "tulip-tree," "liver-leaf," "sanguinaria." It includes names of animals: "wolf," "deer," "bear." The people are named next as the life cycle manifests itself further through the names of things: "The Indian warrior" is killed by other "savage men" with "tomahawks." Next appears an Indian hunter's "lodge," which is "built / With poles and boughs." The "red-man['s]" lodge is hung with the pelts of "wolf and cougar." In this setting "black-eyed maidens . . . / . . . gather . . . / The hickory's white nuts" and the fruit of the "butternut." White settlers enter the scene now with "axe" and "ploughs" to grow "maize" and "buckwheat." The life cycle and human history of the land is told in names. These poems differ from the legend poems, which also name some things uniquely American, in that they establish a clearer context because of the stronger emphasis on the spirit of place.

Three poems of the prairies display Bryant's technique of naming in order to generate an American diction better than any other of his poems. "The Hunter of the Prairies," "The Painted Cup," and "The Prairies" firmly associate American images and themes with the language of the poems. They paint word pictures of the new place to define and characterize the landscape, which becomes for Bryant a metaphor for America. Additionally, "The Painted Cup" and "The Prairies" introduce a unique mythology of the New World in order to establish more firmly the context of the diction and to give a freshness and vitality to the words.

"The Hunter of the Prairies" (1834) names in order to characterize the American place. More than merely cataloging the images and themes that Bryant attaches to the prairies, it connects the themes to the images. It breaks down the imagery of the landscape to the elemental in order to recreate it, thus portraying the new landscape accurately and freshly and suggesting the spirit of place. The themes connected to this new order are American:

abundance and diversity and vastness; freedom; man's relationship with nature; time (particularly the future) and timelessness; the adopted myth of the Promised Land; the country's special mission as suggested by its relationship with God and the connection between the physical and metaphysical realms; and finally, the paradox and ambiguity arising from these themes and from the vast and multifarious new country itself.

The informing principles of the imagery are the four elements—earth, water, air, and fire. The importance of the four elements as a structural device is more completely understood in light of Bryant's comments about Chaos in his second "Lecture on Mythology" (1827). Discussing the role of the elements in the Greco-Roman myths of creation, he first defines Chaos as "that state of confusion in which matter lay before the creation of the universe and of the animated beings that inhabit it." He continues, "Ovid describes Chaos as a mixture of the discordant seeds of things— a jumble of unstable land[,] innavigable water, and rayless air—a war of hot and cold, moist and dry, hard and soft, heavy and light." Bryant then describes a painting of Chaos by Diepenbeke as "a medley of water[,] earth, fire, smoke, wind, etc."[13] The elements are for Bryant the materials necessary for creation. Once things are reduced to their elemental units in his poems of the prairies, then, something new can be created.

First, the flora and fauna in "The Hunter of the Prairies" are associated with the earth. The specific animals native to the prairie are the "red deer," "bison," "elk," "river-fowl," "bear," "she-wolf," "and the brinded catamount" (236–39). Plants that define the land include "bloomy grass," "waving sedge," "elm," "vines," "flowers," "heavy herbage," "dim woods." There are also general references to the earth: "wastes by plough unbroke," "green desert," "pastures," "fresh lawns and shades," "glades," "plain," "woody vale and grassy height." Second, the water imagery consists of "lucid streams," "the vast / And lonely river," "seaward," "founts with rain and dew," "streams," and "tide." References to air and wind are scattered throughout: "pure skies," "fragrant wind," "breezes of heaven," "measureless as air," "the wind." Finally, fire shimmers down as light in a "beam of heaven," but more savagely in stanza 5 it rages as a prairie fire.

The animals, envisioned by the speaker as game and put there by Providence, suggest the adopted American myth of a Promised Land and the conventional themes of the New World's abundance and diversity. Moreover, both plants and animals here connote freedom. The plants that define the prairie also emphasize its ambiguity and Bryant's struggle to incorporate its essence in order to create an American poem. Paradoxically, the trees enclose the prairie by providing its boundaries, yet the "pastures [are] measureless as air." The hunter takes in the "bloomy grass," "waving sedge," and beautiful flowers with his eye. The "blue / Bright clusters *tempt*" him and thus enter his soul (my emphasis). Finally, on a level nearer that of the incorporation of the animals, the "flowers that scent the wind" enter the hunter physically to stimulate his olfactory sense. As the hunter ingests the animals of the prairie and similarly takes in the plants in order to gain the prairie's essence, Bryant uses the names of the animals and plants to capture the essence of the American landscape.

Water is associated with freedom and timelessness. More dramatically, however, astride his horse the hunter "plunges . . . through the tide." This baptism by nature, his rebirth into the prairie's elements, is underscored by a similar baptism by fire. In the fifth stanza the hunter meets this most terrible challenge of the prairie and stands victorious at his cabin door. After this stanza he rhetorically questions the creative force that controls the environment. As the hunter associates "Fire" (note the upper case) with the supreme being, Bryant associates the prairie with the spiritual realm.

The element of air also relates God and the prairie in such phrases as "breeze of heaven." Air further suggests freedom and the unity of sky and land on the prairie, the tenuousness of physical and metaphysical boundaries. Indeed, the air seems as much a part of the landscape as the ground, as this line states in the appositive: "In pastures, measureless as air." The prairie becomes boundless—its horizon line perpetually receding as it is approached. The diction underscores the idea of boundlessness with these words reverberating throughout: "long," "high," "up," "boundless," "vast," "broad," "wide." The denial of and continual extension of the physical boundaries and the union of sky and land offer a metaphoric richness: no boundary—or at most, a very tenuous one—exists between the physical land and the metaphysical sky.

Not all the significant words of the poem are particularly American—nor need they be, nor *can* they be. "Sedge," Middle English in origin, reminds one of John Keats's "La Belle Dame sans Merci." And the use of the four elements as a structural device is certainly not unique to American literature. But the images within this poem are unique to America, and the words sound themes that become, by virtue of their association with the place, particularly American themes.

In "The Painted Cup" (1842) and "The Prairies" (1833) Bryant again reduces the landscape to the elemental. In addition to reconstructing the four elements to paint word pictures, establish the spirit of place, and develop themes, Bryant further Americanizes these poems by introducing in each a new mythology for the new place. In fact, Bryant's reliance on the elements wanes and his attention to mythology increases, his poems here implying the most conventional nineteenth-century definition of mythology. According to Ernst Cassirer, for Friedrich Wilhelm Joseph von Schelling and Georg Creuzer, two of the most influential voices on the study of mythology in the nineteenth century, "all mythology was essentially the theory and history of the gods."[14]

Bryant's concept of mythology is most readily visible in his five "Lectures on Mythology," which he delivered, as Professor of Mythology and Antiquities, to the National Academy of Design in New York in December 1827. He repeated the lectures three times in 1828, 1829, and 1831.[15] His focus throughout the lectures is indeed on the "theory and history of the gods." His first lecture announces the purpose of the series (to show the relationship of classical myth to contemporary American sculpture), and it narrows the focus to the divinities in the myths. Lecture 2 divides the deities into three categories. Lecture 3 addresses the creation of man and stresses the relationship between man and the gods. The fourth and fifth lectures concern Neptune and Vulcan and the gods and goddesses related to them. Bryant's attention in these lectures, then, is on the presence and characters of the gods themselves and on the relationship between men and gods.[16]

Bryant's prairie poems draw on the same concept of mythology. In "The Painted Cup" he is mainly concerned with the spirits that inhabit and reign over the prairie, and in "The Prairies" he celebrates God's hand in the creation of this landscape. The appeal to mythology is the logical extension of Bryant's language experiment, for mythology forms a bridge between the physical and spiritual realms. Revealing the spiritual essence of the new land, the mythology vitalizes the landscape and imparts fresh meanings to the names of the new things.

"The Painted Cup" (1842) opens as "The Prairies" does with a celebratory description of the prairies. The rest of the poem concerns romantic images of fairies and nature gods. The focus of the poem is also double: on the need for a new mythology for the New World and on the poet's role in establishing such a mythology. Emerson thought similarly to Bryant, having written in his journal in 1835, "We need a theory of interpretation or Mythology"—who but a poet, from Emerson's point of view, would be able to provide such a mythology?[17] Bryant's words that help to create the new mythology are, significantly, words particular to the new place, the prairie.

"The Painted Cup" begins:

> The fresh savannas of the Sangamon
> Here rise in gentle swells, and the long grass
> Is mixed with rustling hazels. Scarlet tufts
> Are glowing in the green, like flakes of fire;
> The wanderers of the prairie know them well,
> And call that brilliant flower the Painted Cup. (282)

The fire imagery of the flower merges with the green grass covering the earth, thus associating two elements. At the end of the poem

Bryant associates all four elements: as the *wind* tips the flower to spill its *water*, the strawberry "*breathes* a slight fragrance from the *sunny slope*" (my emphasis). The more important concern here, however, is that the flower is not for slaking the thirst of fairies, nor for "the faded fancies of an elder world," but for the rejuvenation of nature in the New World, the "virgin solitude." The flower nourishes the insects and birds. It ripens the fruit by watering it. It imparts the essence of the prairie.

The prairie, then, requires a mythology separate from those handed us by past, alien cultures. The basis of that mythology is, of course, found in the four elements, since they are universal. But this new myth must be unique to the land, so in the final part of the poem Bryant conjures up a nature god who is related to the native people of the land. The mythical "gentle Manitou of flowers"—his "swarthy worshippers . . . gone," "his rounded cheek all brown / And ruddy with the sunshine"—unseen drinks the dew from the flower on "summer mornings." Manitou is one of the Algonquian deities or spirits dominating the forces of nature. By mentioning his name and showing his action of drinking the dew to incorporate the essence of the prairie, Bryant establishes him as an appropriate being to impart spiritual significance to the prairie. Though he and his worshipers may seem sylvan, they are unique to the prairie and disassociated from English tradition since they are not "faded fancies of an elder world," but are living, inhabiting spirits.

The poem has in its first part described the land, in its second part dismissed the old mythology and recalled the four elements as the basis of mythology, and in its third and last part identified the mythological world of the prairie.

The final comment on this poem must deal with the poet's role in the myth-making process. Bryant begins the second section by addressing himself and American poets in general, much as he speaks to Thomas Cole and all other American painters in "To Cole." In "The Painted Cup" he writes:

> Now, if thou art a poet, tell me not
> That these bright chalices were tinted thus

To hold the dew for fairies, when they meet
On moonlight evenings in the hazel-bowers,
And dance till they are thirsty. Call not up,
Amid this fresh and virgin solitude,
The faded fancies of an elder world. (282)

The new poet of the new land, in other words, must declare his independence from the old myths and allusions if he is in fact truly a poet.

The first solution for Bryant, after dismissal of the old mythology, is to replace it with the *things* of nature that are specific to the prairie. He concludes the second section of the poem as follows:

But leave these scarlet cups to spotted moths
Of June, and glistening flies, and humming-birds,
To drink from, when on all these boundless lawns
The morning sun looks hot. Or let the wind
O'erturn in sport their ruddy brims, and pour
A sudden shower upon the strawberry-plant,
To swell the reddening fruit that even now
Breathes a slight fragrance from the sunny slope.
    (283–84)

This replacement in turn yields a new myth. "But thou art of a gayer fancy," he begins the third and final section, in opposition to the first lines of section two—thus implying that the physical world of the prairie is itself better than the older myths. Furthermore, on a metaphorical level the prairie's god of nature, Manitou, is more inspiring than the matter of conventional, inherited myths. This "gentle Manitou of flowers," specifically of the painted cup, unites the physical and metaphysical. Drinking from this prairie flower, he nourishes himself, incorporates the very essence of the prairie, and joins in communion with his realm. The significant, ceremonial ingestion at the end of the poem—the last phrase is "drain the gathered dew"—asserts the importance of the act. It is spiritual.

The prairies have risen to the metaphysical level. Spirits are not of past legends here, not from remembered times. They coexist with the physical. Physical has conjoined metaphysical on the prairies, as sky meets land, as rain or light or wind comes down from the heavens. The new American poet has named—identified the essence of—the new place, and he has identified himself with the new place and the new mythology. It is the poet's task, Bryant implies, to interpret in the appropriate words and images the "spirit of place." So doing, the poet vitalizes the language as he creates a metaphor for America and its poetry.

"The Prairies" (1833) is the most significant of Bryant's prairie poems quite simply because it is the best, thematically and technically. It catalogs the names of the indigenous plants, animals, and people, as do other of Bryant's prairie poems. These specific images of the prairie establish the context and identify the poem as uniquely American. Though the poem draws on the stock Edenic myth of the New World,[18] it also uses elemental imagery as a foundation for a new mythos, a new diction, and a new metaphor.

"The Prairies" is a self-conscious poem. Phrases echo throughout it to announce that one of its subjects is poetry itself—specifically American poetry. Bryant immediately establishes that the "speech of England has no name" for the prairies. But the speech of America does.[19] It is an American language—a composite language—that will proclaim his American landscape. Furthermore, the inspiring winds of the new poem are "Breezes of the South!"—no conventional English western wind, but a "fresher wind."[20] In part 2 of "The Prairies" the things of nature themselves are speakers, and the language is more closely linked with the American land. In the final section Bryant returns to the present, and the prairie has a particular voice then, too: the insects, birds, and bees fill the "savannas with murmurings." The future voice of the prairie rises from these murmurings as "The sound of that advancing multitude / Which soon shall fill these deserts." These self-conscious references state that here is a poem in a new language, one based on the elements of the landscape, on *its* past, present, and future.

Bryant begins to establish this new language by painting a word picture of the new place. He depicts the prairies in their vastness. They are "the unshorn fields, boundless and beautiful." They are an "encircling vastness" that stretches "in airy undulations, far away," like the ocean. He then details the picture by naming the places of the prairie and its boundaries, by cataloging the flora and fauna, and finally by naming the human inhabitants of the prairie.

After filling in the background with broad images of the new landscape, Bryant puts the borders on his picture with place names. The names are boundaries and landmarks that establish the geography of the new place, and in that sense they give existence to the new place. Most importantly, they are not English words. "Mexico," "Texas," and "Sonora" identify the area with Spain rather than England because of the Spanish rule of Mexico. "Texas" and "Mexico," both native American words, catch the original "spirit of place." "Prairie" is French, whereas "Pacific" echoes both French and Spanish and "bison" echoes German and French. It is likely, then, that Bryant wishes the language of his poem to reflect the variety of this new world, rather than to be limited to the English. The third section of the poem again cites new places—the "Rocky Mountains," "Missouri's springs," "pools whose issues swell the Oregon." While Bryant's expanding diction uses place names to define the geographical area, it also asserts the polyglot language of America.

Adding finer lines and details to his picture of this panoramic landscape, Bryant names the flora and fauna. To name the boundaries of the place is a beginning, but to populate the place with life delineates it and gives it character. The flowers are of course important to Bryant because the prairie is, after all, characterized mainly by the grasses and flowers. The flowers here are "golden and . . . flame-like." Their "glory" and "multitude / Rival the constellations!" Their gaudiness in the final section matches that of the insects. "The high rank grass" is mentioned only once, and the word *rank* suggests the large size of the grass, its coarseness, its fecundity.[21]

Of the animals on the prairie, the "prairie-hawk" is a strong image. It is associated specifically with this American place, and it soars above in the heavens with a majesty and power that are representative of the union of the physical and metaphysical. Other minor animals fill in the background: the prairie wolf and gopher in section 2; the beaver in section 3; the insects; "gentle quadrupeds"; birds; "sliding reptiles of the ground, / Startlingly beautiful"; the deer; and the bee. Though the bee, Bryant says, comes from the Old World, this opposition helps to establish by contrast that all the other animals on his list are uniquely American.

The bison are significant because they represent a truly unique large life form on the prairie. Bryant mentions them twice. In the first instance he suggests that the bison were tamed by the moundbuilders:

> These ample fields
> Nourished their harvest, here their herds were fed,
> When haply by their stalls the bison lowed,
> And bowed his manèd shoulder to the yoke. (186)

The second reference is equally prominent:

> Twice twenty leagues
> Beyond remotest smoke of hunter's camp,
> Roams the majestic brute, in herds that shake
> The earth with thundering steps—yet here I meet
> His ancient footprints stamped beside the pool. (188)

Both references imply the majesty of this largest animal on the prairie, and both suggest a life that is unique and primitive. Both, however, also paradoxically foreshadow the ultimate end of the various forms of being on the prairie. This most American image, and word (by virtue of its connection with the unique animal), is the central animal image of the poem.

The human inhabitants are also unique. The Mound Builders' extinction ensures their particularity. Extinction is also the implied fate of the red man and of the white man, since the "forms of being" continually change. The mounds—word and image—add an Americanness, since they are unique to the landscape of the prairie. They are not merely lumps in the earth, but mounds constructed by a particular race. The image of the mounds represents human life on the prairie: the mounds hold the bones of the past race; they boast the old religion of the Mound Builders; they commemorate the battles and struggles for life on the prairies. The race that has supplanted the Mound Builders, the "red man," is also unique to the geography and represents, therefore, another facet of the American landscape. Unlike the Mound Builders, whom Bryant characterizes as farmers and stock keepers, the red men are hunters, "warlike and fierce." The red men, who leave the prairie for the Rocky Mountains, "a wilder hunting ground," invest the prairies with the spirit of the wild. It is in one era a farmed and controlled land, in the next a wild land, and in the approaching one controlled again. While the land's special characteristics are interpreted through the races that dominate it at various times, the overall picture, the picture through time, is of a diverse landscape—alternately wild and tame.

To further delineate the character of the prairies, Bryant also reduces things to their elemental components, though not to the extent he does in his other prairie poems. Still, the emphasis on the elemental helps him portray the landscape and lay the groundwork for a new myth. The elements suggest a universal quality, but they are redefined as they take on particular associations and as they express the quality of the landscape.

The references to water are necessarily few. The most notable is the comparison of the prairie grass swaying in the wind to the undulations of the ocean, an image that recurs in the metaphor of the "island groves." Thus the prairie takes on the conventional figurative significance of the ocean as the source of life and as the symbol of soul or psyche. The rivers are only incidentally mentioned (line 43), and the other water actually on the prairie is implied when Bryant mentions the beaver, which has moved away. The rivers, the streams in which the beaver used to live, and the pools beside which Bryant sees the footprint of the bison provide some contour and stamp of life as they suggest the theme of the disappearing wilderness.

Finally, the boundaries of water extend the land surface of the poem. Bryant is concerned with more than Illinois, rather with the entire United States (and Mexico), when he speaks of the waters known to the southern breezes: the "brooks / That from the mountains of Sonora glide / Into the calm Pacific" (184).

Fire enters with the sun and metaphorically with the "flame-like flowers," the painted cup of the later poem. When thinking of the dead of the past, Bryant asks, "and did the dust / Of these fair solitudes once stir with life / And burn with passion?" (186) The association of fire is first with the flowers of the earth and then with the spirit of man, as if the prairie has imbued the flower and the man with this element and its corresponding emotion. That quality is ultimately debilitated, but nonetheless adopted, by the inhabitants of the prairie, for the final reference to fire is obliquely through the "smoke of hunter's camp." The passion given by the prairie to the flower and the native human being is perverted by the encroaching, inevitable presence of the white hunter as the passion of the fires is clouded by the dirty smoke.

References to the earth characterize the prairie most completely. Frequent naming of flora and fauna of course suggest the nurturing quality of the land and its abundance. The poem opens with a celebration of the land's beauty and boundlessness. The land itself seems to undulate as "Dark hollows seem to glide along and chase / The sunny ridges" (184). The ground becomes most important in the second section of the poem. As the speaker rides over the earth, he thinks of the dead who are buried beneath him. While he does not develop this theme in the same way that he does in "Thanatopsis," Bryant makes the earth the container of the past, its sepulcher. The land is also associated with three specific themes in relation to the Mound Builders. As noted earlier, it is a place of worship, burial, and protection.

The earth is also a voice at the opening of section 2: it answers Bryant's questions about the past. By the end of the poem the implication of the earth being a graveyard of the past is inverted, and the earth becomes the voice of the future:

From the ground
Comes up the laugh of children, the soft voice
Of maidens, and the sweet and solemn hymn
Of Sabbath worshippers. The low of herds
Blends with the rustling of the heavy grain
Over the dark-brown furrows. (188–89)

The most significant images of the land, however, are the ones that blend the land and sky together. In lines 11–15 it is the movement of the clouds' shadows cast on the earth that creates the illusion of the land itself moving. By the end of the first section, that relationship takes on great religious significance. The Creator has shaped these lands, which are "Fitting floor / For this magnificent temple of the sky" (185).

Images of the element of air, as in the above two examples, emphasize the spiritual quality of the prairie, the more so since sky and land are so closely linked on the prairies. The prairies "stretch / In airy undulations." With his theme of the changing "forms of beings" Bryant associates "the quickening breath of God," which gives life to or takes life from the different forms that have inhabited the prairies. Insects, birds, and bees flutter and murmur to unite the land with the air and sky. It is the bee's hum in the air in which Bryant hears "The sound of that advancing multitude / Which soon shall fill these deserts." Indeed, this sound in the air gives way immediately to the sound "from the ground" of children's laughter, the "soft voice / Of maidens," and the "solemn hymn."

The wind is also Bryant's muse. At the end of the poem the wind disturbs his dream, or vision. It is also the wind that has induced the vision. Bryant begins the poem by describing the prairies poetically, but he gives them no spiritual significance aside from the implication of the ocean metaphor. After celebrating the southern breeze that brings the prairie hawk, however, he explicitly associates the prairies with the Creator and ends the section with the image of the ground as floor and the sky as ceiling of a temple.

With the setting reduced to the elemental and populated with the actors of the new mythology, Bryant can sketch the beginnings of a myth. The Mound Builders, extinct in the present of the poem, have given their place on the prairies to the red men, who in turn give theirs to the white men. This cycle is the core of the myth. It draws on legends of the past in order to explain man's place in the present and to project him into the future. The mythos confronts a specific race's, or culture's, origin and end. The voice of the poem also individualizes these beginnings and endings, and so the poem confronts the mystery of a single person's birth and death, setting them both in relation to the landscape, the microcosm. This voice in turn extends itself to the mythic through the stories of the Mound Builders, the "solitary fugitive," the red men, and by implication, the white men. The speaker unites and embodies them all. The mythic quality of the poem develops what Bryant saw as mythic themes: the relationship between man and the gods, and the presence of the gods in the background. The first section of "The Prairies," in fact, suggests an invocation, at the very least an acknowledgment, of the spiritual power that imbues the prairies.

Unlike the myth in "The Painted Cup," the myth in "The Prairies" relies heavily on a remembered time, not a present time. The memory is, however, of the New World's past, not Europe's. Bryant does allude to the inherited myths of New Eden, New Canaan, and the golden age, but he does so, not so much to assert them as myths of the New World, but to establish this as a myth-making poem.

"These are the gardens of the Desert" immediately echoes the myth of the Promised Land. "I behold them for the first time," proclaims Bryant, in order to extend this myth to the Edenic: as a poet he sees them personally for the first time, but figuratively he is the first man to see them. That God presented this land to man, as he did Eden and Canaan, is the implication at the end of the poem's first section, which celebrates God's role as creator.[22] The myth is underscored at the end of the poem when the poet imagines the "sweet and solemn hymn / Of Sabbath worshippers" in the future raised in praise of their God, their deliverer to these lands. The stories of Genesis and Exodus, however, are not the only mythic allusions. The poet claims that a race of people existed on the prairies "while yet the Greek / Was hewing the Pentelicus" (186). The reference to the bee hiding his honey, "as in the golden age," also alludes to a pre-Judeo-Christian mythology.

Both the Judeo-Christian and Greek mythologies are subverted, however, by the new myth of the prairies when Bryant introduces the popular nineteenth-century concept that a race of people existed on the prairies before the Indians.[23] This mythic tendency comes through most clearly in his imaginative legend of the warrior who crosses from the culture of the defeated race to the culture of the conquerors. After the war between the Mound Builders and the succeeding Indians, a warrior of the first culture is succored by the second culture, and he adapts to their way of life. The elder race is deposed, and the cycle can repeat.

Doubtless, the language in this section and the quality of the tale owe something to Bryant's early reading of Homer when preparing himself for entrance into college.[24] Bryant's Greco-Roman allusions, then, are on one level mere convention. Bryant even further subordinates those allusions. The reference to the Greeks "hewing the Pentelicus" is in a subordinate clause; the main clause proclaims that a race of people existed on the prairies then. The reference "as in the golden age" is similarly subordinated to the common bee hiding his honey. Such subordination asserts the new myth of the prairies. Furthermore, while the Judeo-Christian allusions to Eden or a New Promised Land are scattered throughout the poem, the legend of the Mound Builders and the "solitary fugitive" in the camp of the conquering hunters is sustained through most of section 2. This mythic legend of the New World comprises a full third of the poem. Bryant, therefore, does not assert the dominance of the inherited mythologies of Eden, Canaan, and Greece. Rather, he presents them to establish his as a myth-making poem, a metaphorical interpretation of America and its poetry.

Bryant recognizes that his diction is closely associated with England, so in the introductory section of "The Prairies" he substantially divorces his poem from the English tradition. He opens the poem in defiance of the "speech of England." Interestingly, the first published version of "The Prairies" (1833) includes the line

"For which the speech of England has no name." In 1834 Bryant removed the line, but saw fit to return it in 1836 and leave it in all subsequent editions.[25] He also removes the line referring to a pre-lapsarian world—"The beauty of the earth ere man had sinned—" —thus intentionally diminishing the Edenic allusions in the poem.[26] This diminution demonstrates that Bryant does not want the inherited myths of the Old World to eclipse the new myths of the New World. Evidently, he intended to sound a new poetic language. Bryant ends the first section by comparing the prairies to the hills of the East. Though the reference is to American geography, its implication is that the farther west one moves, the less English influence one finds. So when he hails "The great heavens," "A nearer vault, and of a tenderer blue, / Than that which bends above our Eastern hills," he emphasizes the separation he wishes to make between America and England. He accomplishes this separation first by breaking the landscape down to its elements and then by reconstructing it, by portraying and naming the things of the new place. Thus his diction—a polyglot language appropriate to the vastness and diversity of America—takes on the essence, the spirit, of the place. That job begun, Bryant can use his new poetic diction to promulgate the mythology of the New World—a mythology that reciprocally further characterizes the New World and further shapes its language. The self-consciousness shows that his technique is a deliberate artistic act, as does his acknowledgement of the American muse, the "fresher wind." Through this act of art Bryant is, as Whitman claims about him in *Specimen Days,* "pulsing the first interior verse-throbs of a mighty world."[27]

As Denis Donoghue notes, Bryant wavered "between two traditions—an English tradition, strong in its purposes, and an American tradition just barely emerging into form."[28] His prairie poems testify to his helping to form an American poetry. Although Bryant wrote in English and was influenced by Wordsworth, he knew the value of originality and the dangers of imitation. He wrote in his fourth lecture on poetry, "On Originality and Imitation" (1825), of the faults resulting from too heavy a reliance on a poetic model:

The student, instead of copying nature with the aid of knowledge derived from these models, has been induced to make them the original, from which the copy was to be drawn. He has been led to take an imperfect work—and all human works are imperfect—as the standard of perfection, and to dwell upon it with such reverence that he comes to see beauties where no beauties are, and excellence in place of positive defects. Thus the study of poetry, which should encourage the free and unlimited aspirations of the mind after all that is noble and beautiful, has been perverted into a contrivance to chill and repress them. (*Prose* 1:40)

Perhaps Bryant could not sustain his original voice throughout his poetry, but when it does reveal itself, it is particularly important. "The Prairies," as his most extended effort at creating a new language, establishes itself as Bryant's quintessential American poem. The landscape and language of the prairie, then, represent a new direction for the American poet. "The Prairies" is a poem in a language that, as Bryant put it, "has grown up . . . among a simple and unlettered people; [that] has accommodated itself, in the first place, to the things of nature." With the naming begun, the language can more readily accommodate itself . . . "to the things of art" (*Prose* 1:34).

"The Prairies" is the earliest superior poetical treatment of the American prairies. Compared to other contemporary lyrics about the prairies, "The Painted Cup" is also a skillfully crafted poem. While Bryant's letters about the prairies display his ambivalence and the resulting vision and revision of the creative process, the poems themselves show the culmination of that process. Bryant's experiences on the prairies and the resulting poems offer insight into how a geographical place becomes a poetic metaphor. The poems develop the metaphor of the prairies until it encompasses, not only the nationalistic themes and images of America, but also the genesis of a uniquely American poetry. The metaphor, in the private voice of Bryant's letters and in the public voice of his poems, contains the creative process itself, and it develops the themes, images, native mythology, and language that are available to the public American poet. Indeed, one of the most popular and revered poets in America at the time, Bryant plows the artistic ground for future cultivation.

# CHAPTER THREE

# TILLING, SOWING, AND CULTIVATING
## Popularizing the Prairies

**POEMS BEFORE BRYANT'S "THE PRAIRIES"**
In his 1790 *Miscellaneous Works of Colonel Humphreys*, Colonel David Humphreys included "Western Emigration," a poem that lauds the progress of America, depicting burgeoning towns and "rich Commerce" on "brighter plains, . . . Where fair Ohio rolls."[1] Because of his interest in poetry and the open West, Bryant might have noticed this reference, but it is more likely that he was acquainted with James Kirke Paulding's *The Backwoodsman* (1818), a long narrative poem that linked the prairies to the "idea of the West" and the hope for a better life.[2] Coauthor of *Salmagundi* (1807) with Washington and William Irving, Paulding was also a popular literary figure in his own right, as is evinced by his *Diverting History of John Bull and Brother Jonathan* (1815), which was, according to William Charvat, "probably the first American literary work to be stereotyped."[3]

*The Backwoodsman* tells the story of a man and his family who move west after suffering a life of poverty in the East. Though they have their fears about the wilderness and though they face vengeful Indians in the West, the family is finally rewarded with freedom and prosperity in their new home on the banks of the Ohio river. Before they travel west, they put their faith and hope in the prairies, which are bountiful:

> 'Twas said that o'er the hills, and far away,
> Towards the setting sun, a land there lay,

> Whose unexhausted energies of soil
> Nobly repaid the hardy lab'rer's toil;
> Where men were worth full twice their weight in gold,
> And goodly farms for almost nought were sold;
> Prairies of flowers, and grassy meads abound,
> And rivers every where meander round. (19)

After this passage, which includes the only use of the word *prairies* in the poem, Paulding emphasizes the "Independence" and "Hope" that the West represents. The West also holds fears, however, in the forms of wolves, bears, and "the bloody Indian" (22). Oddly, though the prairies hold future promise, the family must clear the land of trees before putting its cabin up. This puzzling contradiction of a wooded prairie is an example of Paulding's ignoring realistic detail in favor of conventional Eastern Seaboard imagery and themes.

The following simile from *The Backwoodsman*, however, suggests some influence on Bryant's "The Prairies." Shawanoe, a vengeful Indian, is inciting other Indians to rise against the whites in order to obtain retribution for past wrongs:

> As fire new lighted in the dry rank grass,
> From side to side like lazy lightnings pass,
> So did his words inspire the list'ning train,
> Rouse every heart, and light each kindling brain. (98)

Paulding's wording, "dry rank grass," is very close to Bryant's in "The Pairies"; moreover his image, like Bryant's later one, is not merely descriptive but figurative. Though Bryant had intended in 1819 to publish a review of *The Backwoodsman* in *The North American Review*, he could not get a copy of the book. Nonetheless, he was certainly aware of it and had thirteen years before writing "The Prairies" to locate it, which he probably did, considering that he was a friend of Paulding and even collaborated with him on *Tales of Glauber-Spa* (November 1832) before going to Illinois and after returning.

Other poets, such as Sarah Louisa P. Smith of Michigan,

John Finley of Indiana, and William Leggett of Illinois, also wrote poems before 1833 that mention prairies.[4] Of these Leggett is noteworthy because he is the one who recognizes the figurative possibilities of the image and because he very likely influenced Bryant's conception of the prairies. After leaving Illinois in 1822, Leggett became assistant editor of the *New York Evening Post* under Bryant, working for Bryant between 1829 and 1836—a significant period because during that time Bryant's brothers moved to Illinois and Bryant himself visited there. Leggett was also one of the collaborators on *Tales of Glauber-Spa*. Most likely Leggett told Bryant of his experiences in Illinois, and more significantly, because they both wrote poetry, they probably discussed the poetic use of the prairies. Such a discussion is particularly likely considering that Leggett uses the prairie image figuratively in his poem "Lines Written on Leaving Illinois, Aug. 29, 1822." Land and sky in this poem suggest the major metaphorical significance of the prairied landscape—its nearness to the metaphysical realm, its nearness to God. About his two sisters who died in the West, Leggett writes:

> Beneath the prairie turf they lie,
>     And sweetest wild-flow'rs deck the sod;
> Their spirits soar beyond the sky
>     In sweet communion with their God.[5]

Micah P. Flint, son of the western novelist Timothy Flint, published "The Mounds of Cahokia" in his father's *Recollections of Ten Years in the Mississippi Valley* in 1826. Written about the Indian burial mounds near Cahokia, Illinois, mounds similar to those Bryant writes of in "The Prairies," the poem also figuratively associates the sky with the mounds and develops at length another major theme of the prairie metaphor (as does Bryant's poem)—the past when the Indians flourished on the prairies. The prairies become a monument to the Indians in the last stanza of Flint's poem:

> Farewell; and may you still in peace repose.
> Still o'er you may the flowers, untrodden, bloom.

And gently wave to every wind, that blows,
Breathing their fragrance o'er each lonely tomb,
Where, earthward mouldering, in the same dark
    womb,
Ye mingle with the dust, from whence ye rose.[6]

John Howard Bryant, William Cullen's brother, opens "A Sketch," which was printed in *The Illinois Monthly Magazine* (September 1831), with a brief description of a prairie setting:

'Twas summer in the land: thick leaves and flowers,
Tall grass and grain were on the lap of June,
The yellow sunlight trembled on the hills,
The dewy hills fresh with the breath of morn;
And o'er them smiled the golden summer skies.[7]

Having moved to Illinois in 1831, John was William Cullen's main link to the prairied West. And though all of the Bryant family, except William Cullen, eventually moved to Illinois, John remained William's main correspondent in Illinois. The two obviously had a congenial relationship, in part because of their mutual interest in poetry, the topic of poetry being not uncommon in their letters. "A Sketch" testifies to their sharing of poetic ideas and techniques because it obviously draws on William Cullen's "Inscription for the Entrance to a Wood" (1815), both poems portraying the forest as a place to retreat from the strife of the world and to gain an inner peace. It is not unthinkable, then, that William Cullen, in turn, borrowed some ideas from John for his own prairie poems.

## OTHER POEMS FROM THE PRAIRIES

Prairie poems written after the appearance of Bryant's "The Prairies" are easily represented by a few examples, for they all read much the same. Part of the reason that the poetic use of the prairie image becomes so conventional is its popular appeal, an appeal evinced by the circumstances of Matt Field's prairie poetry. The *New Orleans Picayune* commissioned Field to write prose and verse about his summer on the Santa Fe Trail in 1839. His poems abound with the conventional images and themes of the prairies.[8]

Some poems by the western and newspaper poets who are found in nineteenth-century anthologies clearly demonstrate the popularized and conventionalized uses of the prairie image, as well as demonstrate the influence of Bryant, whose "The Prairies" was widely and continually published. Alvin Robinson, who made his home in Chicago, echoes Bryant's reference to "breezes of the South" that "pass the prairie-hawk" and that have "played / Among the palms of Mexico." In "Summer on the Prairies" Robinson writes that "two pilgrim birds," who are flying northward, "tell of isles in a southern sea, / And the shores of Mexico."[9] In "The Western Pioneer" John J. Piatt of Indiana writes about the vision of future "domes of cities vast," an image that compares with Bryant's vision of the civilized prairies.[10] Two other similarities exist between Piatt's and Bryant's poems: the bees are the first pioneers, and the future white emigrants will displace the Indians. Isaac H. Julian's poem "The True Pacific Line" is about the movement of America across the prairies to the West Coast.[11] Not only is it similar to Bryant's earlier poem in its theme of America's western advance and in its mention of the Pacific, but it is also similar to Whitman's later idea of America's fullest expansion to the shores of California.

J. K. Mitchell's poem "The Song of the Prairie" is a good introduction to and summary of the prairie poems written by newspaper and magazine poets for a few reasons. First, Bryant included Mitchell's poem (which was earlier anthologized in Rufus Griswold's 1848 *The Poets and Poetry of America*) in his edition *Selections from the American Poets* (1874). Second, the quality of the poem is representative. Finally, Mitchell packs nearly all the conventional prairie images into this fifty-six-line poem. The poem begins:

> O! Fly to the prairie, sweet maiden, with me,
> 'Tis as green and as wide and as wild as the sea:
> O'er its soft silken bosom the summer winds glide,
> And wave that wild grass in its billowy pride.

> The city's a prison too narrow for thee—
> Then away to the prairies so boundless and free:
> Where the sight is not check'd till the prairie and
> > skies,
> In harmony blending, commingle their dyes.[12]

These two stanzas manage to mention the nurturing "bosom," the wildness, the sea, grass, winds, freedom, boundlessness, union of sky and land, and unchecked sight (which is close to Bryant's lines: "the dilated sight / Takes in the encircling vastness"). Mitchell continues by listing the names of animals and plants that appear on the prairies: fawns, bison, eagle, prairie hen, mockingbird, katydid, prairie rose. It is typical of this type of poem, too, that all these images are left undeveloped. Again echoing Bryant, who says that the "speech of England has no name" for the prairies, Mitchell faults England too: "Let England exult in her dogs and her chase— / O! what's a king's park to this limitless space!"

John Bryant's prairie poems written after his brother's "The Prairies" introduce a less idyllic, but not uncommon, conception of the prairies—the idea that they needed to be controlled and overcome before they could reveal their true beauty and worth. In "The Emigrant's Song," for example, the West is a "vast and desolate plain" to be crossed before the emigrants reach their home on the Pacific coast.[13] "The Maples" demonstrates the speaker's control over the landscape:

> 'Tis six and forty summers,
> > Since the naked prairie land,
> With the slender forest saplings,
> > Was planted by my hand. (102)

Although "Then and Now" glorifies the natural beauty of the prairie covered with flowers, it focuses on the strength, fortitude, and perseverance of the settlers:

> Though scant at first our homely fare,
> A little industry and care,

Soon brought abundance, and to spare;
And the whole land was filled amain. (181)

The prairies, to this man who lives on them, need to be cultivated before they can supply their abundance, and through the obstacles they present they prove the worth of the people living on them.

The ambiguousness of the prairies is further suggested by two poems that deserve to be compared here in their entirety because together they express the duality of the prairie. The first represents the typical laudatory poem written by a westerner, while the second shows that not every westerner shared this exuberance about his environment. B. F. Stribling's poem is titled "Illinois":

> A country in the distant west
> With fertile soil is largely blest
> With prairies spreading wide;
> In summer time full dress'd in green
> Like meadows large, they may be seen
> With blossoms deck'd in pride.
>
> Here Nature's gifts are lavished wide
> Profusely as an eastern bride
> With gems be-spangled o'er;
> And when the sun to rest retires
> And smothers out his radiant fires,
> By us is seen no more.
>
> In slumbers sweet he dreams all night
> Of beauteous scenes that caught his sight
> This country trav'ling o'er;
> And when he wakes at break of day
> On golden cars he rides away
> To view this land once more.
>
> He calls up then the moon his bride
> And down he sits near by her side
> And takes her by the hand;
> If ever I shall cease to run

And be to earth a radiant sun
I'll settle in this land.[14]

M. H. Jenks's "Farewell to Illinois" posits an opposite perspective:

Illinois, adieu to thy flies and mosquitoes,
    Thy black, muddy roads, with their soil three feet
        deep;
I was anxious to gaze on thy beautiful features,
    But in parting I feel no desire to weep.

Farewell to thy dark green alluvial ocean,
    Thy rank waving tall grass and cattle in herds;
Thy "fever and ague," creating emotion
    Expressive of feelings much louder than words.

I passed o'er thy valley by day and nocturnal,
    Thy sun made my head ache, thy moon gave a
        chill;
And I now write it down for my friends and the
    Journal,
    'Tis my first and last visit, let what happen will.

I had heard of thy beauty, been told of thy treasures,
    Of thy wild game and wild flowers "blushing
        unseen";
I long had been anxious to taste of thy pleasures,
    Forgetting that pleasures were followed by pain.

Adieu, Illinois! and to all thy pale livers,
    Thy lily-faced ladies and yellow-skinned men,
I entered thee smiling, and leave with the shivers;
    Let other folks love thee, but I never can.[15]

Jenks also draws on all the conventional imagery, but with a refreshing sense of humor that shows he recognizes the clichés of prairie poetry. The earth is not a garden, but a sucking mud hole. Jenks adeptly reverses Bryant's connotations of "rank," which here become pejorative rather than positive. The entire poem, further-more, recalls accurately some of Bryant's opinions about the prairies as he records them in his letters.

As Jenks's poem shows a change in the use of the prairie landscape, so does the poetry of H. and John Hay. The lyrics of H., a poet who lived in Springfield, Illinois, during the early 1830s, are noteworthy because he lived on the prairies at a relatively early time and because he wrote many poems about the landscape and the culture that existed on it. An English immigrant, H. is known only by this initial, which he used to sign poems that he contributed to Springfield's *Sangamo Journal* from 1831 to 1846.[16] Publishing in the *Sangamo Journal* during that time, H. is significant to this study because he wrote prairie poems both before and after the first ap-pearance of Bryant's "The Prairies" and because of his twofold contribution to the prairie metaphor. First, his contribution lies in the dialect and vivid characterization that are demonstrated best in his satires. Second, and most important, H.'s contribution lies in the duality he depicts in the prairie landscape.

Some of H.'s best poems are satires, and some of these are written in Scots dialect—most likely because of the poet's liking for Robert Burns. The prairie figures significantly in two such poems. "Hame's the Best Place A'ter A'" (published Decem-ber 1831) is a brief narrative about Satan's,—"Auld Nickie-ben's"—journey to and stay in Springfield, where he hopes to find a better life and more followers than in Hell. The shrewish prairie wife whom Satan marries in Springfield and the severe cold of the harsh environment, however, drive Satan back "hame" to Hell. Satan is obviously characterized as strong-willed in the beginning of the poem but, compared to the prairie dwellers, weak-willed at the end. The most complete characterization in the poem, how-ever, is that of the speaker. He is the one who portrays the harsh-ness of Satan's wife and of the landscape, and his control of the entire narrative—and of the character delineation—is under-scored because Satan speaks in the same Scots dialect as the speaker of the poem. Thus the dialect emphasizes the character-ization of the speaker.

Another satire in Scots dialect, "To 'The Prairie Bard'" (January 1832), was actually written to John Howard Bryant, who lived in Jacksonville at the time. Here the dialect obviously helps to characterize the speaker. He finds a kinship with the Prairie Bard, "his rhymin' brither," yet he also jests about the Prairie Bard's town. That Jacksonville has an inn pleases the speaker because, as he says, "I love gude cheer." Such a man would mock, with a light irony, Jacksonville's temperance. He says,

> in your town nae man gets drunk,
> Nor can be found a single punk.
> Heigh, sirs, that I could say as much
> For Springfield, but I can't—in dutch![17]

Later the speaker mocks that temperance has advanced so far in Jacksonville that the ladies have given up their tea. After this banter, the speaker states his purpose in writing to the Prairie Bard—"That we maun all our spunk display / Our common country to embellish" (83). The dialect throughout the poem complements well the vivid character delineation of the speaker.

Though H. introduces a dialect into prairie poetry that is not the dialect of the frontiersman, the dialect nonetheless suggests the backwoodsy, rugged, and pluralistic quality of the prairies. It also helps characterize the speaker as a certain type of prairie dweller— the adventurous European immigrant who wishes to better his lot in life. Indeed, it is this characterization that is one of H.'s most significant contributions to prairie poetry.

H.'s other major contribution is his development of the dualistic nature of the prairie landscape. While he writes some conventionally laudatory prairie poems, H. also writes about the harshness of the prairies, and in a much more serious tone than in "Hame's the Best Place A'ter A'."

"The Western Wilds" (March 1832) is a conventional defense of the prairied West, and as such, it is laudatory. Written in response to Lydia Huntley Sigourney's "The Western Emigrant," it claims that the "western wilds" are not "sad," but gay. The following stanzas are representative:

> Behold our prairies spreading wide;
>> In spring how green they be;
> The gallant steeds that o'er them ride,
>> Away, exulting free!
>
> And he who strides the gallant steed
>> A deeper joy must know,
> With heaven's own blue above his head,
>> And earth's bright flow'rs below! (115)

In a tone as gushing as this (nearly half the stanzas end in exclamation points) the poem's forty-eight lines manage to include nearly all the conventional prairie images and themes. While "The Western Wilds" wholly expresses a positive view of the prairies, poems like "Bards and Reviewers," "On the Arrival of the First Steam Boat," and "Winter Nights" contain numerous references that express a similarly complimentary view.

Other poems, however, depict the duality of the landscape. "To 'The Prairie Bard,'" for example, necessarily draws on prairie images. H. suggests to "The Prairie Bard," his "rhymin' brither," that they both keep their "fancy on the wing," that they

> Describe the blooming prairie green,
> As first in summer it is seen,
> Deck'd out in flow'ers o' golden sheen;
> When earth seems blended with the sky,
> And the keen hawk is circling high,
> Like death aroun' us hovrin' by.
> Then mark what solemn thoughts inspire
> To see our prairies a' on fire;
> Or far off in the wilderness,
> At midnight hear the wolf's distress. (83)

Though the passage is rife with conventional prairie images, H. also introduces the ambiguousness of the prairies by first noting the glorious qualities of the landscape and then noting the negative qualities. The fire and the wolves contrapose the flowers and the sheen of the prairie. But most significantly, the hawk connotes death, a connotation that contradicts the conventional association of hawk and freedom, an association that William Cullen Bryant makes later in "The Prairies." "Vernal Musings" (June 1832) reflects a similar ambiguousness, celebrating the beauty of the prairie and simultaneously lamenting the displacement of American Indians from their land (another topic that becomes conventional and that William Cullen Bryant develops more fully in "The Prairies").

The ambiguousness inherent in the landscape is a predominant theme in the entire body of H.'s prairie poems. Opposing the poems that celebrate the prairies are poems that clearly and forcefully depict the foreboding and destructive qualities of the prairies. The two references to the prairies in "Hame's the Best Place A'ter A'" do not allow full development of the worse-than-hellish quality of the landscape, but the poem certainly adds that dimension to the metaphor. "A Night on the Prairie" (May 1833) recounts a sleepless and fearful night spent without shelter. Poems like "The Exile" (May 1832), "Sonnet" ("There is a charm in foreign lands to be" [June 1838]), and "Il Melancolico per Amore" (June 1832) associate loneliness with the prairie and depict the prairie in comparison to civilized European countries as a natural and cultural wasteland.

Among the foreboding qualities of the prairie is its severe weather, a topic that concerns a number of poems. Harsh rain and snowstorms plague the prairie dwellers and travelers, and the mud of autumn is particularly distressing. The extreme heat of summer is the subject of "Travelling the Prairie in Summer" (July 1832) and "Sonnet" ("Fierce overhead the fervid dog-star reigns" [August 1832]), both of which depict a traveler at the mercy of the prairie sun. The sestet of "Sonnet" is the most forceful description:

> Now one wide blaze of heat beams all around;
> No zephyr stirs the air, no breezes blow.
> The traveller faint, with eyes that seek the ground,
> Moves on his course, irresolute and slow;
> And every living thing, by heat opprest,
> Seeks some cool cover for a place of rest. (136)

"Lines on the Approach of Winter" (January 1832) associates the extremes of winter on the prairie with death:

> Now the wild prairie to the view
> Appears in autumn's sober hue—
> And, past her summer's flow'ry pride,
> Looks like some lone and widow'd bride—
> 'Till at last, advancing cold,
> Another season we behold,
> And instead of lively green
> The winding sheet of winter's seen.
> Now piercing winds, and driving hail,
> The weary, wandering wretch assail—
> Who hails with joy the friendly light
> That guides him in his course aright. (117)

"Wolves" (January 1846) combines the threat of winter with the threat posed by wild animals. As night descends, a lone traveler begins to panic: he "plunges through the snowy waste, / . . . / Till down he sinks at last, and black despair / Brings hideous shapes and fancies to his eyes" (121). As the traveler lies in the snow in terror, the wolves approach, "ready to devour" him. Finally, as the traveler calls to heaven "in vain," the environment mocks his situation ironically:

> No help is nigh—to heaven he calls in vain—
> While the pale moon, as if to mock his woe,
> Shines calm and cold upon the pallid scene. (121)

These last lines, as they call attention to the mockery, connote not simply a disinterested environment but a malevolent one.

H.'s most significant contribution to prairie poetry is his thorough depiction of the prairie's dualistic nature. While John E. Hallwas is right in saying that H.'s poems lack "metaphoric complexity," his poems do attest to his broad range in depicting the various moods and figurative associations of the prairies.[18] H. goes beyond the simplistic depiction of the prairie as completely benevolent. He also avoids the opposite extreme of depicting it as completely malevolent, which is what his countryman Charles Dickens does in *American Notes for General Circulation* (1842). Rather, H. catches both extremes in poems like "Winter Nights," "Vernal Musings," "To the Frogs," "Sonnet" ("Still lingers winter; and the blust'ring wind"), and "Sonnet" ("The sullen hours on leaden pinions fly"), and he adequately covers the moods and attitudes toward the prairies that exist between those extremes. H.'s connection to William Cullen Bryant also invites speculation. Though no evidence exists as yet to show that the two met—much less discussed the use of the prairie image in poetry, it is certainly intriguing to think that they did meet. After all, H. wrote "To 'The Prairie Bard'" for John Howard Bryant in January of 1832, the year William Cullen visited Illinois. One wonders how much Bryant's "The Prairies" owes to H.

Another Illinois poet and the most popular midwestern poet of the nineteenth century, John Hay, also explores the use of prairie dialect and prairie characters in the 1870s. Though he wrote some conventional prairie poetry, notably "Centennial" and "The Prairie" (1858, essentially a catalog of conventional prairie images), Hay also published *Pike County Ballads and Other Pieces* in 1871. The *Ballads* both celebrate and joke about life and people on the Illinois prairies. They add dialect, local color, and fuller character development to prairie poetry. As do H.'s prairie poems, they also depict the dualistic nature of the prairies.

The topics of the *Pike County Ballads* range from the antics of four cronies who pledge temperance for one year in "The Pledge at Spunky Point: A Tale of Earnest Effort and Human Perfidy" to the vocal defense of a crippled black man's right to membership in the community in "Banty Tim (Remarks of Sergeant Tilmon Joy to the White Man's Committee of Spunky Point, Illinois)." Collectively, the various topics of these poems reveal life on and the people of the prairie frontier. The two poems that most directly concern the prairie are "Little Breeches" and "Benoni Dunn."

"Little Breeches" is the story of a young boy aboard a runaway wagon in a deadly Illinois prairie snowstorm. The boy's father, the speaker of the poem, introduces himself:

> I don't go much on religion,
>     I never ain't had no show;
> But I've got a middlin' tight grip, sir,
>     On the handful o' things I know.
> I don't pan out on the prophets
>     And free-will, and that sort of thing,—
> But I b'lieve in God and the angels,
>     Ever since one night last spring.[19]

This simple faith and down-to-earth candor characterize the morality of the frontier people of Pike County.

Later in the poem, the father's acceptance of the boy's fate in the storm demonstrates the pioneers' acceptance of natural phenomena. Finding the horses and wagon, but not the boy, the search team assumes that Little Breeches has wandered off, got lost in the storm, and succumbed to the harshness of the prairie. The sky darkens, and the men, knowing of a sheepfold nearby, retire there for the night. As the reader expects, they find Little Breeches there, warm and comfortable among the sheep and innocently oblivious to his dangerous situation. The father ends the poem by asserting that the angels guided the boy to the fold:

> And I think that saving a little child,
>     And fotching him to his own,
> Is a derned sight better business
>     Than loafing around the Throne. (9)

The dualistic prairie has the power to kill or return the boy. Because Little Breeches remains innocent, however, and because the father accepts his son's fate, Little Breeches is spared. Neither father nor son is in conflict with his environment, but each is sympathetic— even empathetic—with it.

While "Benoni Dunn" is not collected among the *Pike*

County Ballads, it is in subject, mood, and setting very much a Pike County ballad. A monologue spoken by Benoni Dunn, a poor prairie farmer from Pike County, the poem delineates the opposite type of prairie dweller from that of "Little Breeches." Dunn's philosophical musings are framed by the voice of the speaker, who is sitting on a fence talking with Dunn. The speaker establishes the setting in stanza one:

> Prairie and timber were glorious
>     In the love of the hot young sun,
> But a philosophic gloom possessed
>     The soul of Benoni Dunn. (225)

After this introduction, Dunn immediately asserts his philosophical position: "Nothin' in all this 'varsal yerth / Is like what it ort to be" (225). Dunn believes that everything in this world works according to the principle of inversion:

> The weaker a feller's stummick may be,
>     The bigger his dinner, you bet,
> And the more he don't care a damn for cash,
>     The richer he's sure to get. (225)

Because the world functions according to this principle, Dunn need not work himself. The implication of his philosophy is: working will not lead to gain; not working, conversely, will lead to success.

Dunn reiterates his principle in stanza five:

> Everything works contrary—
>     You never knows what to do:
> Ef I sow in wheat I'll wish it was corn
>     Afore the fall is through.
> And talk about pleasure—ef I was axed
>     The thing that most I love,
> I'd say it's gingerbread—and that
>     I git the littlest uv. (226–27)

Dunn makes the wrong choice about what to plant and, unwilling to accept responsibility for his choice, is dissatisfied with the results. He loves gingerbread, but will not make himself any. Instead, he expects to "git" it without any effort. Dunn is never rewarded, so, filled with regret and hate, he develops his cynical philosophy.

The speaker closes the poem with this condemnation of Dunn:

> And this was the sum of the thinking
> Of tall Benoni Dunn,—
> While gay in weeds his cornfield laughed
> In the light of the kindly sun.
> Ruminant thus he maundered,
> With a scowl on his tangled brow,
> With gaps in his fence, and hate in his heart,
> And rust on his idle plough. (227)

Dunn's unattended field (in "weeds" of mourning, if we recognize the ironic pun), broken fence, and rusty plow speak loudly against him. He is shiftless. He has, in part at least, brought his bitterness on himself.

This character sketch of Benoni Dunn, however, is more than an exposé of a lazy farmer. The poem does not simply suggest that man is the cause of his own problems on the prairie. Dunn is beaten, in part, by his environment. Because of the combination of personal laziness and a disobliging environment, he can come to no other conclusion than to give up: "'I've give up tryin' to see the nub—/ It's too hefty a job fer me'" (225, 227), he states twice in the poem. The prairie setting established at the beginning of the poem and the images of the cornfield, the fence, and the plow at the end are strategically placed clues to indicate what has beaten Dunn. These opening and closing images in the poem stress man's relationship to the prairie, particularly his need to cultivate it. The prairie is a hard environment to tame, however: it demands constant labor with specially fashioned tools. It will stake its claim on the human who tries to work it.

The humor of "Benoni Dunn" somewhat mitigates the extent to which Dunn is harmed by the prairie environment. His comic monologue and character indicate that he is not totally destroyed by the exacting landscape. Nonetheless, the prairie has forced him to adopt his cynical philosophy—which will keep him inactive and check any tendency he may have to work in order to better his circumstances.

Of course, the prairie could not harm Dunn if he had more fortitude and perseverance. The prairie at its most severe does not destroy Little Breeches because he remains innocent and because his father accepts his son's fate. As Dunn strives against his natural situation—through his philosophy of experience, cynicism, and nonacceptance—he is overwhelmed by the prairie. According to Hay in these poems, the prairie is in itself neither cruel nor malevolent, but dualistic. The harsh and unaccommodating prairie separates the weak-willed from the strong-willed pioneers. It separates those individuals empathetic with it from those inimical to it.

Many of these poems by prairie poets suggest Bryant's influence and identify "The Prairies" as the first noteworthy poem about this landscape. Most importantly, these poets demonstrate the extent to which the prairies had become popular as subject matter for American poets and their audiences. Thus they testify to the importance of this landscape as a poetic device that could help to make American poetry unique. H. and John Hay, especially, emphasize this important poetical use of the prairies. Their attention given to dialect, to character development, to local color, and to the dualistic nature of the prairies unearths more of the metaphorical significance of the prairies.

## NATIONALLY RECOGNIZED POETS

Oliver Wendell Holmes is remembered primarily as an occasional poet, one who could produce on demand poetry adequate to the celebration of a situation or person. As a genre occasional poetry does not allow the fullest display of poetic powers, and Holmes's references to the prairies occur in such poems. Still, these poems are adequate to the situation, and they introduce a formal device that Whitman more fully realizes—placing the image of the prairie at the center of the poem, reflecting the central geographical region of the continent.

"America to Russia" (1866), written to commemorate a diplomatic mission, was read by the "Hon. G. V. Fox at a dinner given to the Mission from the United States, St. Petersburg."[20] In ten ballad stanzas the poem celebrates the link between these two nations. Beginning at stanza 6, approximately at the center of the poem, is the mention of the prairies, whose "garnered store" does *not* fill the "sunless hold" of the ship bound for Russia. Instead, the cargo of the ship is a "people's love." Holmes also mentions another freight that is *not* on the ship, "rich Nevada's gleaming ore" (199). As one of only two geographical areas of the United States mentioned in the poem, the prairies become representative of America. Though less valuable than the love of the American people, they stand for the abundance of America, a wealth at least equal to the nation's silver and gold. Central to the geography of the United States, the prairies are both structurally and figuratively central in the poem.

In the first stanza of "At a Dinner to General Grant" (1865) the prairies are listed among other landscapes, including fields, "east and west," and "coast and hill and plain" (205). Being about the gathering of men from across the United States during the Civil War, this poem refers to these men as the "harvest," a suggestive word when one considers the association of abundance and the prairies in "America to Russia." The prairies are again figuratively central to the poem because the personage of Grant, who came from Ohio, looms large in the background, as the only person capable of leading the northern forces.

James Russell Lowell wrote only one poem—but an important one—that concerns the prairies, "The Pioneer" (1847). A romantic poem, lauding the life in nature that allows man to be completely free, "The Pioneer" is in a sense an anomaly among Lowell's poems.[21] Emersonian in concept, it depicts nature as man's release from the constraints and strictures of society. Each stanza posits a rhetorical question about man's preferences in life. Collectively, the gist of the questions is this: What man would live constrained by city and society when he could live free in the expanses and beauty of nature?

The first stanza, while positing the rhetorical question that is the focus of the poem, emphasizes the importance of the prairie image, contrasting the freedom implied by the prairie with the strictures of urban, Eastern Seaboard society:

> What man would live coffined with brick and stone,
>     Imprisoned from the healing touch of air,
>     And cramped with selfish landmarks everywhere,
> When all before him stretches, furrowless and lone,
>     The unmapped prairie none can fence or own?

The importance of the image of the prairie is reiterated at the end of the second stanza, where Lowell emphasizes the boundlessness of the natural frontier:

> What man would read and read the selfsame faces,
>     And, like the marbles which the windmill grinds,
>     Rub smooth forever with the same smooth minds,
> This year retracing last year's, every year's, dull traces,
>     When there are woods and un-penfolded spaces?[22]

After this beginning, Lowell develops the themes of solitude, discovery, self-reliance, change and hope, and freedom. All are represented in the natural landscape, which the prairie introduces and, because of its expansiveness, encompasses.

Lowell further intermingles these themes to suggest the richness of their interrelationship by using two poetic techniques: the antithetical structure of his poem and the sheer number of images he uses. The two stanzas quoted above demonstrate how Lowell introduces the opposition between city and nature: he first maligns the city, then praises the wilderness. That pattern of opposition within each stanza continues until stanza 6, which in its entirety emphasizes hope and change. Next, the first line of stanza 7 praises nature, and the rest of the stanza disparages the city. Because they oppose the pattern of stanzas 1–5, stanzas 6 and 7 constitute the turn of the poem. The whole of stanza 8 then derogates society, and the wholes of stanzas 9 and 10 extol life in the wilderness. The whole poem, therefore, reiterates the pattern of each of the first five stanzas. Lowell stresses the opposition between city and nature within the structure of each of the first five stanzas, and then in the turn of the poem, stanza 6, suggests the larger structure of opposition between the stanzas themselves. The first five stanzas of the poem are, in fact, rhetorical questions, and the last five stanzas can be considered the answer. The first five stanzas, that is, ask why one would live in the city, and the last five stanzas answer that one should live in nature.

Lowell is equally deliberate with the intermingling themes and images. The first stanza juxtaposes the confinement of the city with the openness of the prairie. Three images suggest the social confines of the city: the polluted air, and the monuments and edifices that are "selfish landmarks." Society constructs its own prisons of the spirit, buildings separating man from the "healing touch of air," in its cultural structures. The second stanza plays on this same opposition, but now the constraints, intellectual and spiritual stasis, are put into abstract terms suggestive of mind and time—such abstraction extending the figurative import of the poem. The third stanza offers other images to develop the constraint of intellectual stasis; the fourth, images of spiritual stasis. Stanza 5 introduces the moral corruption that limits man in society. The images that represent these themes of social, intellectual, spiritual, and moral degeneration include, in addition to the ones cited from stanzas 1 and 2, the study of books, creeping toward Lethe, and pushing and altercating amid a crowd.

Images of nature are also interwoven in the first five stanzas. Among them are the images of the prairie and "unpenfolded spaces," which carry with them a number of themes, including meditative solitude, discovery of unmapped places, and limitlessness of spirit and potential. Images of open spaces also reflect the themes of self-reliance and strength. These images and themes then recur throughout the rest of the poem and culminate in a celebration of the great American theme of freedom.

Like Bryant's "The Prairies," Lowell's "The Pioneer" is a rendering of the popular themes of a nationalistic nineteenth-century American poetry. Lowell's other comments on the prairies and the West in general, however, show that this poem popularizes ideas about the West that he may not fully believe. In "A Fable for Critics," for example, he implicitly disparages the prairies. Criticizing James Fenimore Cooper's portrayal of women, Lowell writes that they are "all sappy as maples and flat as a prairie."[23] While on an 1855 lecture tour of Illinois and Wisconsin, in a letter to Charles Norton dated April 6, Lowell degrades the West, writing that it is "the East over again—only dirtier and worse-mannered."[24]

Lowell's metaphorical use of the prairies in "The Pioneer" remains, nonetheless, a complex and artistically competent one. Precisely because the poem is an anomaly among Lowell's poetry and because he does not fully believe what he has written in it, "The Pioneer" forcefully acknowledges the extent of the prairie's popularity in American poetry. Moreover, Lowell's poem serves as a précis to Whitman's expansion of the same subject matter in "Pioneers! O Pioneers." Though one might argue that Lowell's poem commends the peaceful coexistence of man and nature, while Whitman's celebrates man's dominance over nature, the poems are linked by more than the titles. Whatever the character differences between the pioneers in these two poems, in both works it is the relationship with the prairied West that gives man his sense of spiritual fulfillment.

Alice and Phoebe Cary, who published their poems in newspapers and magazines and collected them in a number of popular editions, add a new dimension to prairie poetry—the role of women on the prairies. Having been born in the Miami River Valley, about eight miles north of Cincinnati, and having lived there about thirty years (until 1850), the two sisters had firsthand experience of life in the West. Though they write conventional prairie verse as far as some of their prairie themes and images are concerned, they emphasize the figure of the woman.

Alice's conventional poem "Abraham Lincoln" makes some associations that Whitman also draws on in "When Lilacs Last in the Dooryard Bloom'd." The prairies cover Lincoln in death, so he, an emblem of freedom and hope for America, becomes associated with that landscape. Because he is also "born of the people," Alice Cary, again like Whitman, lets Lincoln and "his own loved prairies" represent the common, average American.[25] Phoebe Cary's poem "John Greenleaf Whittier" also makes a conventional reference to the prairies, identifying the prairies with the sea and with the great expanse of America, which she claims is Whittier's poetical domain. Whittier is "In every home an honored guest— / Even from the cities by the sea / To the broad prairies of the West" (401).

Phoebe emphasizes the family in "The Prairie on Fire," a poem about the threat of a grass fire to some emigrants in a covered wagon. Though the poem opens with pictures of the father and boys, the image of the mother and the little children serve as significant counterpoint. The wife is "sweet" and "patient, / With the babe on her breast," yet she is obviously under strain since she "sees their new home in fancy" and "longs for its rest" (416). When the family recognizes the blaze and understands the danger, the children cling to the mother for security. But she is equally terrified, as the last lines show: "the mother and children / Are weeping for joy" after they have escaped their seemingly imminent doom (417). The wife's imagining her new home complements Annette Kolodny's theory in *The Land before Her* of the West being for pioneer women largely an imaginative place and experience.[26] According to Cary, for women the ideal of the West remains "fancy," whereas the hardship is reality.

Phoebe's other prairie poem, "The Lamp on the Prairie," is a ghost story, the center of which is a mother who awaits her son's return. Since her son left home thirty years ago during a snowstorm and has not returned, the woman lives alone in a cabin on the prairie. For thirty years she has kept a lighted candle in the window to guide her son. At the end of the poem she believes he is outside, and the wind, "or a hand unseen," opens the door (325). The woman falls across the threshold and dies, thinking that her son has returned. After her death, every midnight a candle appears in her cabin window. Cary relies upon the mystery of the prairie setting to add to the eeriness of her tale. But the emphasis throughout is on the woman's isolation and the hardship and loss that she has faced on the prairie.

Alice Cary more directly confronts women's hardship on the prairie frontier in "The West Country." After beginning the poem with an image of beauty by associating the homes on the prairie with "birds' nests," Cary turns her audience's stock responses around by calling attention to the emotional losses and hardships the women suffer:

> Have you seen the women forget their wheels
>     As they sat at the door to spin—
> Have you seen the darning fall away
>     From their fingers worn and thin,
> As they asked you news of the villages
>     Where they were used to be,
> Gay girls at work in the factories
>     With their lovers gone to sea!

The "bird's nests," then, as Cary reverses the connotations, become a most appropriate simile because of their fragility and exposure. At the end of the poem, however, Cary reconciles herself to the suffering by finding comfort in the role and accomplishments of the women.

> Of the little more, and the little more
>     Of hardship which they press
> Upon their own tired hands to make
>     The toil for the children less:
> And not in vain; for many a lad
>     Born to rough work and ways,
> Strips off his ragged coat, and makes
>     Men clothe him with their praise. (208)

The women's accomplishments are in rearing *lads* who will become praised by *men*. Alice Cary confronts the reality of women's existence and the limits of their aspirations on the prairie frontier.

The first American woman to support herself and her children by writing poetry, Lydia Huntley Sigourney published, among her eighteen books of poetry (including reprints and collections), *Select Poems* (1847) and *The Western Home, and Other Poems* (1854). Though she did not live in the West, Sigourney drew upon the themes and images associated with it. In *Select Poems* she writes about the difficulties of the pioneers and also about the displaced natives in such poems as "The Western Emigrant," "Death of the Emigrant," "Our Aborigines," and "Indian Names." Unlike the Carys, Sigourney does not stress the role of white women in the West. Rather, she emphasizes the difficulties faced in the wilderness by Indian women.

"Indian Girl's Burial," set on the Wisconsin prairie, is representative of Sigourney's prairie poems in its display of the degraded position into which the whites have forced the Indians. About the burial of an eighteen-year-old girl whose death is being mourned by her mother, the poem focuses on a native woman of the prairie. As the mother wails by her daughter's grave, "Pale faces gather round her, / . . . / But their cold, blue eyes are dry" (*Select Poems*, 146). The whites spurn the woman because "she was an Indian mother," and the death of the girl does not affect them because "she was an Indian maiden" (147). The portrayal acknowledges the hardships of native life on the prairie—both the hardship of the wilderness that takes life and the cultural hardship caused by the advance of the whites onto the prairie.

The title poem of *The Western Home* touches on a similar theme. The baby of an emigrant couple is dying, and the mother receives commiseration and some solace from the experience and story of a native woman. The Indian woman with her baby had escaped a massacre by Colonel Williamson in which all other Indians had been killed. Though the mother tries to survive with her baby in the wilderness, the baby dies and the mother lives the rest of her life near the baby's grave.

"Oriska," which is set on the prairies, is also a poem about the ill treatment of the Indians by the whites, and the sufferer is again a woman. Oriska is a Sioux Indian who has married a Frenchman. Though she is devoted to him, he eventually leaves her and their son. After a lengthy period of grief, Oriska searches for her husband. When she finally finds him, he is married to a white woman, and he sends Oriska away as if their former relationship were of no consequence and as if Oriska has no feelings nor validity as a human being. Oriska then drifts over Niagara Falls in a canoe with her son clinging to her in terror.

The theme of the displaced Indian is not original in Sigourney—in the early 1820s Bryant wrote "An Indian at the Burial Place of His Fathers." Nor is the topic in "Oriska" original—also in the early 1820s Bryant wrote "Monument Mountain." Sigourney, however, specifically uses a prairie setting, having thereby, in a sense, moved "Monument Mountain" to the prairies. Furthermore, unlike Bryant, whose "Monument Mountain" remains purely romantic, she focuses on some real hardships confronting native women in a way similar to the Carys' focus on the hardships facing emigrant women.

Though, like Sigourney, John Greenleaf Whittier never visited the West himself, he wrote a number of poems that use a prairie setting, and that suggest that his interest in the prairies was greater than Holmes's, Lowell's, the Carys', and Sigourney's. More than any of the other popular poets, Whittier stresses the themes of freedom and democracy by grounding them in the free soil versus slave soil conflict of the day, particularly as the conflict focused on Kansas.

Whittier initially became interested in the prairied West as early as 1822, when he heard about Ohio and Indiana from William Forster, an aquaintance who toured the region in 1820.[27] It was seventeen years later that Whittier first referred to the prairies in his poetry. Three early poems emphasize the prairies: "Ritner" (1837), "Pennsylvania Hall" (1838), and "The New Year" (1839). Whittier also revised "The Pawnee Brave" (1827) in 1842, retitling it "The Rescue." While the early version of this poem has no specific setting, "The Rescue" sets the tale of a Kansas Indian in the prairied West. Cora Dolbee explains Whittier's initial conception of the prairies: "Whittier visualized the freedom that first pressed 'the virgin verdure of the wilderness' in Pennsylvania, as now spreading 'her white pinions to our Western blast' and shedding her strengthening light 'o'er lakes and prairies.'"[28]

"On Receiving an Eagle's Quill from Lake Superior" (1849) nationalistically spreads freedom's "white pinions" over the continent. At the opening of the poem the speaker is brooding on a cold and dark winter day, but the arrival of the gift of an eagle's quill causes his "torpid fancy" to awaken, and he imagines the beauty and grandeur of the West. The lake is the first image to come to his mind, but the prairie that lies next to it enters quickly: "I see, with flashing scythe of fire, / The prairie harvest mown!"[29] Though forest, waterfalls, and rivers are also depicted, the speaker's revery returns to the land itself—significantly, the land of the Mississippi Valley. From the prairied center of America the speaker's imagination rises to the mountains of the West, where he finally salutes the symbol of the eagle, which represents "the ample air of hope" (145). The poem ends with this bright and suggestive image of the symbol for the United States: "The sunshine of the upper sky / Shall glitter on thy wings!" (145) At first enclosed in his room, the speaker has imaginatively brought himself to lake and land, across prairies, up mountains, to the sky.

At the same time that the poem's upward movement suggests the relationship between land and sky and acknowledges the spiritual qualities of the prairies, the poem also follows the movement of American civilization westward. Beginning at the edge of the prairies, the poem moves to the western mountains, then to the western shores. His poem reflects Bryant's "The Prairies" when Whittier writes about the future populating of the West:

> And city lots are staked for sale
>   Above old Indian graves.
>
> I hear the tread of pioneers
>   Of nations yet to be;

> The first low wash of waves, where soon
>> Shall roll a human sea. (145)

Similar to Bryant's poem, too, the future pioneers of Whittier's poem will cultivate the prairie, as the phrase "the prairie harvest mown" suggests.

Unlike Bryant, however, and like Whitman, Whittier continues beyond the prairies. "Westering still," a star is leading the "New World" over mountains to "California's golden sands" (145). In "When Lilacs Last in the Dooryard Bloom'd" Whitman depicts Lincoln as a western star that was a guide for the nation and that now attracts the attention of the speaker. Furthermore, Whittier is writing about the westward movement to California in a way similar to Whitman, yet he is doing it not only before the publication of "Passage to India" but six years before the initial publication of *Leaves of Grass*.

In the 1850s Whittier focused his prairie poems on the theme of freedom versus slavery, and in so doing he politicized the prairie metaphor. Because the free soil versus slave soil conflict focused on Kansas, so did Whittier's poems. "The Kansas Emigrants" (1854), the most popular of Whittier's Kansas poems, establishes the prairies as representative of an American tradition of freedom.[30] Using sea imagery and referring to the past, he compares the pioneers' crossing of the prairies to the pilgrims' crossing of the Atlantic. The poem opens:

> We cross the prairies as of old
>> The pilgrims crossed the sea,
> To make the West, as they the East,
>> The homestead of the free! (317)

The prairie pioneers' relation to the pilgrims is further strengthened in the last stanza, which is a slight revision of stanza 1. Changing "pilgrims" to "fathers," Whittier draws on a familial metaphor to emphasize the tradition of freedom in America. Other slight variations in the last stanza focus attention more definitely on the prairies: instead of *crossing* the prairies as the pilgrims "crossed" the sea, the pioneers "tread" the prairies as their fathers "sailed" the sea. This change implies that some pioneers stay on the prairies, rather than pass over them.

This exchange of the word "tread" for "cross" not only more firmly associates the prairies with freedom; it also stresses the theme of the future population of the prairies. In images recalling Bryant's "The Prairies," Whittier suggests that the pioneers will cultivate and civilize the prairie wilderness, as he does in "On Receiving an Eagle's Quill." They will "plant" the "Mother-land['s]" "common schools / On the distant prairie swells." They will "give the Sabbaths of the wild / The music of her bells." They will "plant beside the cotton-tree / The rugged Northern pine"—a symbol of Northern domination in the free soil versus slave soil conflict (317).

As the prefatory note to this poem states, "The Kansas Emigrants" celebrates "the great democratic weapon—an overpowering majority" (317). Such a majority will ensure that the Kansas territory will remain free and will in the future, through this freedom, realize America's fullest potential. A tradition that began with the pilgrims will be realized on the prairie frontier, which thus becomes a New Canaan.

The cost of this freedom is the topic of a few other Kansas poems by Whittier. "The Burial of Barber" (1856), "A Song of Freedom" (1856), and "Le Marais du Cygne" (1858) portray a prairie that is blood stained. Thomas Barber, a free-soiler who was shot and killed, becomes a "martyr" to freedom, his grave a monument. Similarly, in "A Song of Freedom" the Kansas soil is testimony of the bloodshed:

> The Kansas homes stand cheerlessly,
>> The sky with flames is ruddy,
>> The prairie turf is bloody
>>> Where the brave and gentle die.[31]

The fields become graves—symbols of the evil results of the conflict caused by slavery and of the tribulations suffered by the Kansas supporters of freedom.

"The Panorama" (1856) is a lengthy poem of 520 lines that Lewis Leary calls Whittier's "most comprehensive, and rhetorically most effective political poem."[32] Written in heroic couplets, the poem is literally a "show" of America, its past, present, and future. The speaker is called the "Showman," as it is he who commands that the curtain be raised from the stage and who interprets the present evil of slavery and the possibilities for the future of America. The first scene onstage is a panorama of the prairies:

> At length a murmur like the winds that break
> Into green waves the prairie's grassy lake,
> Deepened and swelled to music clear and loud,
> And as the west-wind lifts a summer cloud,
> The curtain rose, disclosing wide and far
> A green land stretching to the evening star. (324)

After describing the scene further, Whittier suggests the dreamlike and spiritual quality of the prairies, writing that the scene brings

> vaguely to the gazer's mind
> A fancy, idle as the prairie wind,
> Of the land's dwellers in an age unguessed;
> The unsung Jotuns of the mystic West. (324)

Whittier lyrically establishes the prairies as the representative American scene.

Reverberating with familiar images and ideas, the next stanza glorifies the landscape:

> Beyond, the prairie's sea-like swells surpass
> The Tartar's marvels of his Land of Grass,
> Vast as the sky against whose sunset shores
> Wave after wave the billowy greenness pours. (324)

"Beyond" asserts the limitlessness of the landscape. The sea imagery rivals Bryant's, and the connection of earth and sky suggests the "mystic," or metaphysical quality of the prairies.

As Whittier projects beyond the prairies to the mountains and Pacific Coast, he draws on a prevalent nineteenth-century belief that Whitman also develops, particularly in "Passage to India," in which the prairies complete the "Rondure" of the world. The progressivist belief held that "human progress had proceeded westward, from the Middle East [through Europe] to North America"[33] and would complete its cycle by crossing the Pacific to Asia. First, Whittier elaborates on the sea imagery until the prairies merge with the Pacific, which "rolls his waves a-land" (324). Then, he connects the New World with the ancient East: the Pacific, which is now associated with the prairies, becomes the "world's highway" as it opens the trade routes from America to "far Cathay" (324).

With the essential themes of America introduced and America placed in a world history, the Showman begins his interpretation:

> "Such," said the Showman, as the curtain fell,
> "Is the new Canaan of our Israel;
> The land of promise to the swarming North
> Which, hive-like, sends its annual surplus forth;
> To the poor Southron on his worn-out soil,
> Scathed by the curses of unnatural toil;
> To Europe's exiles seeking home and rest,
> And the lank nomads of the wandering West,
> Who, asking neither, in their love of change
> And the free bison's amplitude of range,
> Rear the log-hut, for present shelter meant,
> Not future comfort, like an Arab's tent." (324)

The prairies are here coupled with another pervasive American theme, the founding of a New Canaan, a promised land that can provide for all people. Again, like Whitman, Whittier connects the prairies with the rest of the world—in this instance not only in space, but, through the recollection of biblical history, in time.

Next, the Showman describes a glorious picture of the future, but his description is interrupted by the ugly, present reality of slavery. After the Showman's lengthy diatribe against slavery, which constitutes the last half of the poem, the poem ends with the poet's voice enjoining the reader to "Forget the poet, but his warning heed, / And shame his poor word with your nobler deed" (330). The prairies are, therefore, representative of the situation in America at the time of the writing of the poem (the present). They are representative, that is, of past ideals of American freedom *and* of future promise of freedom. They are the gateway to American fulfillment.

Whittier is an important figure for poetry about the prairie for two reasons. First, he firmly connects the other popular poets with Walt Whitman. Both Whittier and Whitman imply the importance of America's place in a world history in two ways: by associating America's past with its present and with its future potential; and by associating the popular, nationalistic themes and images of the prairies with the reaches of American influence and potential beyond its western shores. Second, Whittier does not merely use the conventional nationalistic themes to write poems that will be popular; he focuses his prairie poems on the slavery versus freedom conflict, taking a firmer political stance than the western and newspaper poets and the other nationally popular poets. Thus he adds to the prairie metaphor the political significance of working for a change in governmental policy.

## LONGFELLOW

Henry Wadsworth Longfellow does not get politically involved, nor does his poetic vision extend past America's western shores. But like Bryant and Whitman, Longfellow is concerned with establishing a national literature. As early as 1825, while a senior at Bowdoin College, he composed and delivered a commencement address titled "Our Native Writers." Though in it Longfellow admits that "we cannot yet throw off our literary allegiance to Old England," he also asserts that "we may rejoice . . . in the hope of beauty and sublimity in our national literature, for no people are richer than we are in the treasures of nature."[34] In the same address he speaks more directly about an American nature that he later draws on in "Hiawatha": "Every rock shall become a chronicle of storied allusions; and the tomb of the Indian prophet shall be as hallowed as the sepulchres of ancient kings."[35] Seven years later Longfellow published in the *North American Review* an essay titled "The Defence of Poetry," which alludes to a new edition of Sir Philip Sidney. Longfellow is no longer as deferential to English literature as he was in "Our Native Writers," and he retains his view that American poets must look for their subject matter and inspiration in their American environment. American poets must, he asserts, write "naturally . . . from their own feelings and impressions, from the influence of what they see around them, and not from any preconceived notions of what poetry ought to be, caught by reading many books, and imitating many models."[36] These ideas are strikingly similar to Bryant's, as expressed in "On Originality and Imitation." The relationship between the Indians and the sepulchres of ancient kings also echoes Bryant's "Thanatopsis," and one wonders if Longfellow is not drawing directly from that poem, which appeared in the *North American Review* in 1817 and in Bryant's *Poems* (1821). Longfellow admits that Bryant influenced him in his early years. In his *Life of Henry Wadsworth Longfellow* Samuel Longfellow, the poet's brother, reprints the following note written to Bryant by Henry Wadsworth Longfellow: "Let me say what a staunch friend and admirer of yours I have been from the beginning, and acknowledge how much I owe to you, not only of delight, but of culture. When I look back upon my earlier years I cannot but smile to see how much in them is really yours. It was an involuntary imitation, which I most readily confess."[37]

Whether or not Longfellow's theory is imitative of Bryant, in "Evangeline: A Tale of Acadie" and "The Song of Hiawatha" Longfellow draws substantially on the American environment—but with a distinct difference between the two works. Though the prairies are a significant landscape in both narrative poems, in "Evangeline" (1847) they serve, as they do for the western and newspaper poets and for much of what the nationally popular poets write about them, merely as a convenient setting. In "Hiawatha" (1855), however, the prairies take on a distinctly metaphorical significance, representing, first, the ideals of Hiawatha and his people and, ultimately, the joining of two cultures that help give America its particular character.

In his biography of his brother, Samuel Longfellow publishes a number of the poet's journal entries about "Evangeline." From one entry scholars have learned that Longfellow referred to particular sources when writing the second part of that poem. On December 15, 1846, Longfellow wrote: "Of materials for this part there is superabundance. The difficulty is to select, and give unity to variety."[38] Murray Gardner Hill has compared passages from the three influential sources to passages from the second part of "Evangeline." Two of the books, J. C. Frémont's *Expedition to the Rocky Mountains* (1845) and Charles Sealsfield's *Life in the New World* (1844), contain descriptive passages of the prairies from which Longfellow apparently drew.[39] Therefore, when Longfellow records in his December 15, 1846, journal entry that the second part of "Evangeline" "fascinates" him, he records his fascination with the prairies. He further records on February 17, 1847, that on this day he "wrote [the] description of the prairies for Evangeline."[40] Revealingly, the same entry includes this note: "Find the ground covered with snow, to my sorrow; for what comes as snow departs as mud." Since his note about the prairies in "Evangeline" follows immediately after this statement, one wonders if he does not make some mental association between the prairies and the desolation of the snow and mud. Certainly, such a desolate tone is appropriate to the second section of "Evangeline," in which Evangeline is separated from her husband, Gabriel, and searches for him on the prairies.

Though Longfellow never saw the prairies, his vicarious experience with them serves his purposes in "Evangeline." Longfellow saw John Banvard's paintings of the Mississippi, which affected him greatly, shortly after he began work on "Evangeline." He notes in his journal: "Went to see Banvard's moving diorama of the Mississippi. One seems to be sailing down the great stream, and sees the boats and the sandbanks crested with cottonwood, and bayous by moonlight. Three miles of canvas, and a great deal of merit."[41] Hardly allowing the prairies to become a metaphor, "Evangeline" remains primarily descriptive, making common associations with the prairies in such phrases as "limitless prairie"; "flowery surf of the prairie"; and "bellowing," "numberless," "wild," and "unclaimed" herds that rush "o'er the prairie."[42] Longfellow's artistic treatment of the landscape is more skillful than that of the other popular poets, however, and his use of these common themes and images evinces a fuller understanding of the prairies' significance. Instead of stressing the positive connotations of the prairies, for example, Longfellow stresses the melancholic connotations.

First, the prairies represent distance, especially distance from a loved one, as when Gabriel, Evangeline's husband, is rumored to be on the prairies. Representing this separation of loved ones, then, the prairies are used to reinforce a melancholy, even dreadful tone.[43] Longfellow compares a "sound of dread" heard by Evangeline to a sound that "startles the sleeping encampments / Far in the western prairies" (83). As Evangeline drifts down the Mississippi with other Acadians, looking for their husbands, wives, and kinsmen, Longfellow emphasizes their emotional desolation with a simile employing the prairie:

> As, at the tramp of a horse's hoof on the turf of the
> prairies,
> Far in advance are closed the leaves of the shrinking
> mimosa,
> So, at the hoof-beats of fate, with sad forebodings of
> evil,
> Shrinks and closes the heart, ere the stroke of doom
> has attained it. (86)

For Gabriel, too, the prairies are melancholy: he has "sought in the Western wilds oblivion of self and of sorrow." Longfellow also underscores the irony of Gabriel's boat passing Evangeline's (during her search for him) on the other side of an island with this somber allusion: "Swiftly they glided away, like the shade of a cloud on the prairie" (87). These ominous references reflect Evangeline's fruitless search for Gabriel, a wandering search that the trackless prairie helps to emphasize.

Though the mood of the prairies is foreboding, the prairies themselves are also beautiful. Their beauty, however, complements their sadness. In "The Philosophy of Composition," which first appeared in *Graham's Magazine* (28 April 1846) while Longfellow was working on "Evangeline," Edgar Allan Poe wrote that the tone of "sadness" was the most appropriate to beauty's "highest manifestation." While I do not contend that Longfellow was directly influenced by Poe's argument, I do wish to intimate that Poe's statement about beauty and sadness is an accurate assessment of popular literary thought and taste at the time, and as such characterizes the relationship between the prairies' beauty and the melancholic tone of "Evangeline." In the poem Father Felician, who accompanies Evangeline on her journey down the Mississippi, is the first to vocalize the beauty of the prairies:

> Beautiful is the land, with its prairies and forests of
>   fruit-trees;
> Under the feet a garden of flowers, and the bluest of
>   heavens
> Bending above, and resting its dome on the walls of
>   the forest.
> They who dwell there have named it the Eden of
>   Louisiana! (88)

This Edenic allusion is too pat to counteract the tone of gloom that otherwise imbues the prairies. Most significantly, this description of the prairies' beauty ends the priest's speech of hope. Trying to comfort Evangeline in her sorrow at having lost Gabriel, he tells her that they will find Gabriel at their destination, the towns of St. Maur and St. Martin. His conventional appeal to hope, however, does not change Evangeline's mood.

Not only is this first reference to the beauty of the prairies interjected amid three other associations of the prairies and gloom, but it is merely a wish, rather than a certainty. In fact, Evangeline and Father Felician do not find Gabriel at those towns; instead, ironically, they learn there that Gabriel has just left and that they must have met and passed by his boat on their journey down river. The stock associations of beauty and hope, therefore, only reinforce the irony and set in relief the gloom of the scene.

The two lengthiest descriptions of a prairie actually seen by Evangeline further emphasize her loss and sorrow. Having found Gabriel's father, Basil, on his ranch in a prairied land, Evangeline wanders around his gardens at night. She passes along the edge of a prairie, her heart "heavy with shadows and night dews":

> The calm and the magical moonlight
> Seemed to inundate her soul with indefinable
>     longings,
> As, through the garden-gate, and beneath the shade
>     of the oak-trees,
> Passed she along the path to the edge of the
>     measureless prairie.
> Silent it lay, with a silvery haze upon it, and fire-flies
> Gleamed and floated away in mingled and infinite
>     numbers. (91)

The beauty of the prairie certainly does not connote joy, but the wild prairie's melancholic atmosphere—strengthened by its eerie, magical mood—sympathizes with Evangeline's heavy heart.

Though this passage relates the prairie to heaven and introduces the physical-metaphysical union on the prairies, again, this is not a positive relation:

> Over her head the stars, the thoughts of God in the
>     heavens,
> Shone on the eyes of man, who had ceased to marvel
>     and worship,
> Save when a blazing comet was seen on the walls of
>     that temple. (91)

Evangeline denies the relationship of the prairie and God, "And the soul of the maiden, between the stars and the fire-flies, / Wander[s] alone" (91). She cries not to God but to Gabriel, and instead of drawing on the prairie's connection to God for comfort, she laments:

> O Gabriel! O my beloved!
> Art thou so near unto me, and yet I cannot behold
> thee?
> . . . . . . . . . . . . . . . . . . . . . . . . . . . . . . . . . .
> Ah! how often thy feet have trod this path to the
> prairie!
> . . . . . . . . . . . . . . . . . . . . . . . . . . . . . . . . .
> When shall these eyes behold, these arms be folded
> about thee? (91)

As Evangeline's denial of the prairie's connection with God enhances the melancholic sense of isolation, the prairie's vastness represents the spiritual void that exists for Evangeline because of her loss and separation from her lover.

After this experience on the edge of the prairie, Evangeline wanders onto the prairies, accompanied by Basil, in search of Gabriel. Longfellow introduces them, and the reader, to the prairies in his most extended description:

> Spreading between these streams are the wondrous,
> beautiful prairies;
> Billowy bays of grass ever rolling in shadow and
> sunshine,
> Bright with luxuriant clusters of roses and purple
> amorphas.
> Over them wandered the buffalo herds, and the elk
> and the roebuck;
> Over them wandered the wolves, and herds of
> riderless horses;
> Fires that blast and blight, and winds that are weary
> with travel;

Over them wander the scattered tribes of Ishmaels'
    children,
Staining the desert with blood; and above their
    terrible war-trails
Circles and sails aloft, on pinions majestic, the
    vulture,
Like the implacable soul of a chieftain slaughtered in
    battle,
By invisible stairs ascending and scaling the heavens.
Here and there rise smokes from the camps of these
    savage marauders;
Here and there rise groves from the margins of swift-
    running rivers;
And the grim, taciturn bear, the anchorite monk of
    the desert,
Climbs down their dark ravines to dig for roots by
    the brook-side,
And over all is the sky, the clear and crystalline
    heaven,
Like the protecting hand of God inverted above
    them. (92)

Here is a compendium of images and themes associated with the
prairies. They are beautiful, bedecked with flowers, abundant with
wildlife, vast and limitless, wild and relentless, and near the heavens.

Yet Longfellow's description of the prairies also captures the
ambiguous nature of the prairies, and that ambiguity overshadows
the prairies' beauty. Longfellow gives equal space to his catalog of
flora and fauna and to his development of the savagery and slaugh-
ter; the prairies are beautiful and gardenlike in their abundance,
yet they are also a blood-stained desert. The vulture, usually consid-
ered ignoble and in this case ironically similar to Bryant's hawk in
"The Prairies" and to Whittier's eagle in "On Receiving an Eagle's
Quill," scavenges the dead on the battlefield, yet is "majestic" and is
"ascending and scaling the heavens." The paradoxical vulture fur-
ther asserts the ambiguity of the prairies because he is "like the soul

of a chieftain" in the metaphysical sky, yet "over all is the sky, . . . / Like the protecting hand of God." The sky connotes the spiritual world of both the natives and the white pioneers. The "protecting hand of God" becomes doubly ironic when one considers that it is spread over a blood-stained desert, "terrible war-trails," and "savage marauders."

Evangeline wanders the prairies, looking for Gabriel, but she does not find him; instead she experiences an enchantment. After she exchanges stories of being separated from their lovers with an Indian woman whom she encounters on the prairies, Evangeline is again filled with dread:

> Filled with the thoughts of love was Evangeline's
> heart, but a secret,
> Subtile sense crept in of pain and indefinite terror,
> As the cold, poisonous snake creeps into the nest of
> the swallow. (93)

The snake enters the garden. Evangeline's fear is "no earthly fear," and she "felt for a moment / That, like the Indian maid, she, too, was pursuing a phantom" (93).

Evangeline never finds Gabriel in the wilderness. Years later, in Philadelphia, she meets him by accident when she is nursing the sick during an epidemic of fever and one of the patients is Gabriel. Their meeting lasts only moments before he dies. Evangeline has left Nova Scotia at the beginning of the story, traveled down the Mississippi, and wandered the forests of Michigan and the prairies in search of Gabriel. When she does not find him until she returns East, we must conclude that the West, and especially the prairies, represents aimless wandering, isolation, and separation.

By drawing on the ambiguous quality of the prairies and inverting the common themes of hope and beauty in order to emphasize the gloom and dread, Longfellow gains a complexity that testifies to his understanding of the prairies' value as an artistic device. Still, in "Evangeline" the prairies chiefly remain a setting that is sympathetic with the heroine's emotions. In "Hiawatha," by contrast, the prairies become a metaphor rather than a backdrop. Though Longfellow had no more personal acquaintance with the settings of "Hiawatha" than he did with those of "Evangeline," his journals again provide insight into his sources for this quasi-epic. He notes his interest in Henry Rowe Schoolcraft's studies of the Indians and in the Finnish epic *Kalevala*, which he used as a prosodic model for "Hiawatha."[44] His reliance on Schoolcraft's work for the subject matter of "Hiawatha" is well documented, and although most scholars fault Longfellow for his unrealistic treatment of Indian life,[45] one offers a tenable explanation for his deviations from myths and actualities. Cecelia Tichi argues "that Longfellow's design for 'Hiawatha' pertains less to his softening of hard truths for the sake of the picturesque than it does to his attitude toward cultural continuity between the old world and the new." He has structured his plot, she maintains, with the intention of working toward a national literature "that would give native American materials some parity with those of Europe, and further make plausible an Indian–Euro-American cultural continuity in America."[46]

The inaccuracies in "Hiawatha," then, rather than indicating Longfellow's inability to appreciate and reconstruct the reality of Indian life, attest to his grappling with the large problems of creating a national literature. "Hiawatha" is thus more than an interesting and popular story that "sold 10,000 copies the first four weeks and 30,000 in six months."[47] Not merely a long narrative poem with an exotic, epic hero and a native setting that corresponds to the hero's moods and actions, "Hiawatha" is itself a representation of what American literature should be, or at least could be, according to Longfellow, and its hero is representative of the force that moves two cultures to unity. The story's setting, therefore, is symbolic of both the birthplace and the culmination of this cultural unity.[48]

In "Hiawatha" Longfellow uses the prairies often in similes, much as the other popular poets do. He draws on the common associations of flowers, grasses, animals, fire, and snow. The lily of the prairie is mentioned often, as is the bison. Fire and snow are also frequently associated with the prairies. Wolves are mentioned once.

Though this type of reference remains superficial, it does make the prairie setting ubiquitous in the narrative.[49]

The prairies' importance is made clear in the introductory canto. The stories and traditions that make up the narrative, the reader is told, are "from the forests and the prairies" (114). Though other places are listed, these two are the broadest, most-encompassing landscapes. Appropriately, the prairies imply unity at their first mention. These stories, which have been told to the narrator by the singer Nawadaha, had their origins in the "lodges of the beaver, / In the hoof-prints of the bison" (114), two images precisely reflecting Bryant's "The Prairies." Furthermore, the prairies are associated with the idea of origins—the origins of the stories themselves in the "text" of nature.

In canto 2, "The Four Winds," the prairies represent even more elemental origins. Because the second canto personifies the winds as spirits, the winds represent spiritual origins. Mudjekeewis, the West Wind, for example, is Hiawatha's father, and Shawondasee, the South Wind, is clearly associated with summer and the prairies. Shawondasee ripens the corn in the tale about the genesis of maize:

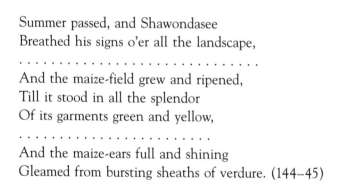

Summer passed, and Shawondasee
Breathed his signs o'er all the landscape,
. . . . . . . . . . . . . . . . . . . . . . . . . . . .
And the maize-field grew and ripened,
Till it stood in all the splendor
Of its garments green and yellow,
. . . . . . . . . . . . . . . . . . . . . . . .
And the maize-ears full and shining
Gleamed from bursting sheaths of verdure. (144–45)

Because in addition to ripening the corn Shawondasee sends the robin, bluebird, swallow, goose, melons, tobacco, and grapes (118), summer's nurturing and abundance are effected by the South Wind, hence by the prairies.

Reciprocally, the prairies affect Shawondasee. Once, while "gazing northward,"

> Far away upon a prairie
> He beheld a maiden standing,
> Saw a tall and slender maiden
> All alone upon a prairie. (118)

Falling in love with this maiden, but unable to tell his love, Shawondasee watches the "maiden of the prairie" (118) as her hair turns from yellow to white. In his sorrow "the South-Wind o'er prairie / Wandered warm with sighs of passion" (119). Though it turns out that Shawondasee was deluded by the "prairie dandelion" (119), this story makes some interesting associations with the prairies. The genesis of the warm spirit winds on the prairies is implied. As in Bryant's "The Painted Cup," therefore, the prairies are inhabited by a spirit that gives significance to the landscape. Furthermore, as in "The Painted Cup," the spirit imparts a passion to the landscape that gives it a character of its own, one that can in turn, perhaps, be imparted to the inhabitants of the land. Finally, this story of the dandelion deluding Shawondasee suggests the enigmatic and ambiguous nature of the prairies.

Further developing the origins of the relationship between the physical and metaphysical on the prairie, the story associates Hiawatha's own beginnings with the prairie. As Hiawatha himself was conceived and born on the prairie, his mother, Wenonah—later called the "Lily of the Prairie"—was born and raised "among the ferns and mosses," "among the prairie lilies," "in the moonlight and the starlight," "on the prairie full of blossoms" (119). Continuing his description of Wenonah's childhood, Longfellow writes that she "grew up like the prairie lilies," "With the beauty of the moonlight, / With the beauty of the starlight" (119).

The West Wind, Mudjekeewis, who has "supreme dominion / Over all the winds of heaven" (117), seduces Wenonah and engenders Hiawatha, and again the link between physical and metaphysical is emphasized:

And the West-Wind came at evening,
Walking lightly o'er the prairie,
Whispering to the leaves and blossoms,
Bending low the flowers and grasses,
Found the beautiful Wenonah,
Lying there among the lilies,
Wooed her with his words of sweetness,
Wooed her with his soft caresses,
Till she bore a son in sorrow,
Bore a son of love and sorrow.
      Thus was born my Hiawatha. (119)

Mudjekeewis eventually grants Hiawatha immortality as the ruler of the Northwest Wind, Keewaydin, the home wind (123). Appealing to the mythic relationship between gods and humankind, as Bryant does, Longfellow closely associates the prairie with the genesis of this demigod.

Because his mother dies soon after his birth, Hiawatha is raised by his grandmother, Nokomis. She teaches him from the text of nature, and the imagery associated with his learning is drawn mainly from the birds, fireflies, stars, and moon. When he first sees a rainbow and asks what it is, Nokomis answers with this final association of prairie and sky:

'T is the heaven of flowers you see there;
All the wild-flowers of the forest,
All the lilies of the prairie,
When on earth they fade and perish,
Blossom in that heaven above us. (120)

Since Hiawatha's origins are in the prairies and since his role throughout the story is to unite the Indian tribes, the prairies also take on metaphorical significance as the center of Indian existence, as the place of union. The main reason Hiawatha courts and marries the Dacotah maiden, Minnehaha, is to unite the Ogibway and Dacotah people. At Hiawatha's and Minnehaha's wedding feast the musician's song celebrates the union of the lyric's speaker and Onaway, "wild-bird of the prairie" (138); thus the uniting of the two nations through this marriage is symbolically related to the setting. More explicitly, the first canto of "Hiawatha," "The Peace-Pipe," announces that unity among the Indians is the poem's central theme. The Master of Life, Gitche Manito, while standing "on the Mountains of the Prairie," "called the tribes of men together" (115). Here Gitche Manito creates a river, a symbol of unity and continuance, and from the "Red Pipe-stone Quarry" of the prairie fashions a peace pipe, the smoke of which rose "Till it touched the top of heaven, / . . . And rolled outward all around it" (115). Prominent in this interpolated story of unity and of the symbolic river's origins are images of the relationship between the prairies and the heavens.

The prairie is, furthermore, the geographical center of the continent. Seeing the smoke from the pipe, the Indians come

> From the Vale of Tawasentha,
> From the Valley of Wyoming,
> From the groves of Tuscaloosa,
> From the far-off Rocky Mountains,
> From the Northern lakes and rivers. (115)

The tribes, from all areas of North America, gather on the central prairie:

> All the warriors drawn together
> By the signal of the Peace-Pipe,
> To the Mountains of the Prairie. (115)

Gitche Manito then tells them his reason for gathering them. He is "weary of [their] quarrels" (116), and he asks them to wash off their warpaint in the symbolic river that he has created. Following this baptism, the warriors bury their weapons and make peace pipes. After the nations are spiritually reborn into a harmonious world on the prairies, in a vision Hiawatha is given his mission to maintain the unity of the nations so they can prosper.

The ending of "Hiawatha" also underscores the spiritual nature of the prairie by comparing it to the sky in a simile. Like Huck Finn and Natty Bumppo, Hiawatha heads West at the end of the story, but he is going to his immortality. Longfellow describes the West in terms of the ethereal sky:

> And the evening sun descending
> Set the clouds on fire with redness,
> Burned the broad sky, like a prairie.
> . . . . . . . . . . . . . . . . . . . . . . . . . . .
> Westward, westward Hiawatha
> Sailed into the fiery sunset,
> Sailed into the purple vapors,
> Sailed into the dusk of evening. (164)

Hiawatha goes, in fact, as Longfellow says in the last line of the poem, "to the Land of the Hereafter" (164). Through this simile of the sky and the prairie and through the metaphor of the West and the Hereafter, Longfellow implies that Hiawatha returns to the prairies, the place of his origin, when he achieves his immortality.

Not only are the prairies in "Hiawatha" geographically and literally central, but they are artistically and figuratively central as well. Beginning "Hiawatha" with clear references to the prairies, including references to the prairies throughout, and ending with a metaphorical allusion to the prairies, Longfellow uses that landscape as a formal center. The prairies are also thematically central to the narrative because they represent the unity of the tribes. Finally, they are spiritually central to the Indians because they are the place where Gitche Manito appeared to them, because they hold such a close relationship with the metaphysical sky, and because they are the place of the genesis of Hiawatha, the demigod whose divine mission it is to maintain unity and guide the tribes to a fuller and more prosperous life.

The growth of Longfellow's use of the prairies from "Evangeline" to "Hiawatha" is a continuation of the metaphor's growth from its use by the western, newspaper poets and the nationally recognized poets. After Bryant published "The Prairies," a sheaf of verse about the prairies appeared in magazines, newspapers, and books. While these verses gain depth from Bryant's meditation, they do not evince the individual author's understanding of the metaphor's richness, as does Bryant's poem. After the appearance of "The Prairies" in *The Knickerbocker* (December 1833), prairie poems in general include more imagery of flora and fauna; they include themes of boundlessness; they make bolder and more frequent associations between sky and land; they develop their images and themes more fully. Yet on the whole, the poems imply that their authors are imitating more than thinking and creating. John Hay and a poet who signed his work simply H., both of Illinois, are exceptions; they do add a new dimension to the prairie metaphor, both using local color and dialect. Collectively, the prairie poems that thrive after 1833 suggest that, as the popularity of the westward movement grew, poets exploited the images of the prairie to write poems that would be accepted by a mass audience, poems that would be printed.

The popularization of the prairies suggests that they are seen by poets and their audiences as something uniquely American. The poets can draw on this landscape, then, and presume that they are writing something new, something appropriate to the New World. The audience is also more readily gratified by the images because such images reinforce the readers' identities as Americans. Nationally recognized poets besides Bryant—Holmes, Lowell, Whittier, the Carys, Sigourney, and Longfellow—also draw on the prairies and further show how this landscape is popularized. As James K. Justus writes about them, "they embodied the aspirations, needs and values of a free-wheeling, activist, expansionist society."[50] As nationally popular poets of their day, they firmly grounded the prairies' place in American poetry.

Not all of these nationally recognized poets, however, display a firm understanding of the richness of the prairies as an American trope. Holmes and Lowell do not make substantive use of the prairie; instead, they make only a few poetic gestures to the landscape—proving the extent of the prairies' popularity, but adding little to the metaphor's depth. Whittier uses the prairies more than Holmes and Lowell, but his use remains focused on the single theme of freedom in opposition to slavery. The Carys and Sigourney briefly introduce the role of white and native women on the prairies into the metaphor and help to emphasize the gloomier side of the metaphor.

With Bryant, Longfellow shares a larger grasp of the metaphor's depth and richness than other popular poets. Though in "Evangeline" the prairies serve mainly as a convenient setting, the use of prairie imagery in that poem is extensive. Common themes and images associated with the prairies help reflect the moods, actions, and emotions of the heroine, and Longfellow shows a fuller understanding of the metaphor in the way he inverts the common connotations of those themes and images and emphasizes melancholy, not hope. "Hiawatha," however, shows more thoughtful and extended use, or cultivation, of the landscape when the prairies, as in Bryant's "The Prairies," assume complex metaphorical significance.

# CHAPTER FOUR

# FROM "REVERY" TO NIGHTMARE
## The Limits of the Optimistic Metaphor in the Private Voices of Dickinson and Melville

Emily Dickinson never saw a North American prairie. She also "never saw a Moor." But as a poet of the imagination, she writes about those geographical areas with more than merely an assurance of their existence or a knowledge of what they look like. Rather, she recognizes her poetic relationship to them, and she develops them as metaphors of the imaginative act of poetic creation.

Poem number 1052 is an aphoristic assertion that imagined experience is as valid as any other, so-called *real*, experience:[1]

> I never saw a Moor—
> I never saw the Sea—
> Yet know I how the Heather looks
> And what a Billow be.
>
> I never spoke with God
> Nor visited in Heaven—
> Yet certain am I of the spot
> As if the Checks were given—

Dickinson equates her knowledge of the moor and sea, of the "Heather" and "Billow," with a Christian faith in the existence of Heaven and God. This equation, which is reinforced visually by the poem's symmetrical, two-stanza design, is her postulate for non-material existence: if one can believe in God and Heaven without seeing them, one can certainly believe in the moor and sea. Dickinson's epistemological statement here asserts that knowledge is a matter of faith. This is not to say that knowledge and Christian faith are synonymous, that knowledge is related to or dependent on a Christian God or any god. Rather, knowledge is contained in the individual consciousness, and once there and regardless of how it got there, it exists—independent of sense perceptions.

The equation in this poem juxtaposes two separate statements—one in the first stanza, one in the second. The conspicuous period at the end of stanza 1—the only conventional punctuation in the poem—clearly distinguishes the images of the two parts. Dickinson offers no grammatical nor verbal connection. She neither states that imagining a moor *is like* imagining heaven, nor that imagining a moor *is* imagining heaven. Instead, her equation identifies two separate acts of the imagination. Neither moor, sea, nor heaven is the focus of the poem. The focus is, in Wallace Stevens's words from "Of Modern Poetry," on "the act of the mind."[2]

Rather than telling the reader how she gained her knowledge about moor, sea, and heaven, the poet declares that she has not "visited" them—that she has not seen these places at all. She does not say, as many readers might assume, that she has seen pictures of moor and sea. The reader is certain only of the poet's knowledge and of how she *did not* gain it. The poet therefore declares a personal faith in her knowledge, as it exists in her mind, of what moor and sea look like and of heaven's existence.[3]

Just as she "never saw a Moor," Dickinson never saw a prairie. But she can make one. She knows the essential component—a specific type of imagining, "revery":

> To make a prairie it takes a clover and one bee,
> One clover, and a bee,
> And revery.
> The revery alone will do,
> If bees are few. (P 1755)

Light-humored as this poem is, it concerns the power to create: the individual, through "revery," can "make" a prairie. Imagination is the only requirement for creating this vast landscape. One need not see a prairie first. Even the clover and bee, which Dickinson uses here as the only concrete images of the prairie, are superfluous.[4] Dickinson *makes* her own metaphor here: the prairie, mostly open space, acquires its significance from the poet's imagination.[5]

In seven poems Dickinson uses the word *plain* to refer to a vast and open geographical area. The plains in these poems cannot always be readily identified with the western plains of America. Because of her familiarity with the Bible, Dickinson could, admittedly, be drawing on its many references to plains. But because she sees "New Englandly" (P 285) in the following poems—"The Wind begun to knead the Grass—" (P 824), "Like Rain it sounded till it curved" (P 1235), "The Day undressed—Herself—" (P 716), and "It sifts from Leaden Sieves—" (P 311)—the plains in these poems connote the American plains. (Because her plains carry many of the same thematic associations as does the general nineteenth-century prairie metaphor, perhaps Dickinson's familiarity with the Bible discloses the source of many of the themes that other poets associate with the prairies.)

In "The Wind begun to knead the Grass" (P 824, first version) *plain* is used to signify the surface of the earth in general. In "Like Rain it sounded till it curved" (P 1235) and "Left in immortal Youth" (P 1289) *plain* assumes negative connotations, as the area is associated, respectively, with remoteness and inferiority. An interesting triple play on the word appears in "The Day undressed—Herself—" (P 716):

> The Day undressed—Herself—
> Her Garter—was of Gold—
> Her Petticoat—of Purple plain—
> Her Dimities—as old
>
> Exactly—as the World—

The day unveils the plain—a place—as the sun dawns over the continent. The day's nobility is clearly and obviously—plainly—

asserted in the color purple. The day's royalty, however, is understated nicely: the color purple in this context is unpretentious, almost common and drab—plain, because it complements "The Day" so well.

The plain is an important figurative landscape in "It sifts from Leaden Sieves—" (P 311), "A Tongue—to tell Him I am true!" (P 400), and "The Mountain sat upon the Plain" (P 975). In these poems Dickinson employs four essential themes of the metaphor: (1) the connection between the physical and the metaphysical; (2) the connection between the material and the imaginative, especially the artistic; (3) time, particularly eternity; and (4) isolation and solitude.

The mountain is representative of deity in "The Mountain Sat upon the Plain," and his "observation [is] omnifold" because he overlooks "the Plain." The plain is, in fact, synonymous with "everywhere." The mountain is a deity, moreover, in another way: "Grandfather of the Days is He / Of Dawn, the Ancestor—." The spiritual connections between the plain and a deity are clearly brought into play.

In "It sifts from Leaden Sieves—" the snow

> makes an Even Face
> Of Mountain, and of Plain—
> Unbroken Forehead from the East
> Unto the East again—

The snow has a leveling power that brings the face of the world, both mountain and plain, full circle from morning horizon to morning horizon. If we recognize the figurative reference to Christ in Dickinson's repetition of "the East," the leveled mountains and plains are associated not only with the physical sky but with the metaphysical realm of heaven, a spiritual association reinforced in the poem when Dickinson writes that the snow "deals Celestial Vail."

"It sifts from Leaden Sieves—" also develops the connection between materiality and the artistic imagination. The snow is an artist, creating, like the poet, its own structures. While Dickinson's association of snow and art may derive from Ralph Waldo Emerson's poem "The Snow-Storm" (1846), her poem is unique in that it associates the snow's and poet's art with the plain. The snow in Dickinson's poem does not merely and literally fall from the sky. Rather, poetically and figuratively

> It sifts from Leaden Sieves—
> It powders all the Wood.
> It fills with Alabaster Wool
> The Wrinkles of the Road—

At the end of the poem (and like the end of Emerson's poem) the falling snow vanishes, as does the poet, and leaves only its artistic creations:

> It Ruffles Wrists of Posts
> As Ankles of a Queen—
> Then stills its Artisans—like Ghosts—
> Denying they have been—

The power of the snow to create, to make "an Even Face / Of Mountain, and of Plain—" is like the imaginative power of the poet to capture thoughts in words.

"A Tongue—to tell Him I am true!" develops the themes of eternity and solitude or isolation. Dickinson again levels the landscape, but this time the leveling is not creative, but destructive. She associates the plain with the heavens and with deity, albeit with the ending of those metaphysical entities. The psychologically tormented speaker of the poem distractedly communicates her fidelity to a lover. Instructing a messenger to convey her devotion, the speaker ends:

> Say—last I said—was This—
> That when the Hills—come down—
> And hold no higher than the Plain—
> My Bond—have just begun—

And when the Heavens—disband—
And Deity conclude—
Then—look for me. Be sure you say—
Least Figure—on the Road—

The leveling and the association of plain, heaven, and God are apocalyptic. Though the speaker's devotion will last an eternity, longer than the hills, indeed longer than God himself, what will remain is a solitary figure on a vast plain. However negatively, the poem associates the plain with time and solitude.[6]

Dickinson reveals her knowledge about a specific *prairied* West and its metaphoric import to America in three letters, which span a period of twenty-seven years. On March 5, 1853, she ends an impassioned letter to her sister-in-law, Susan, lamenting Susan's absence, by associating the West with her "flood subject," Eternity: "I . . . stand and watch the West, . . . the golden West, and the great silent Eternity, for ever folded there and bye and bye it will open it's everlasting arms, and gather us all—all" (L 103).[7] In two letters to Thomas Wentworth Higginson, she uses the word *prairie* specifically. The first reference appears in a February 1879 letter congratulating Higginson on his second marriage (L 593). The word *prairie* is in the title of a book that Higginson's wife, Mary, had published in 1877, *Seashore and Prairie*. In an August 1880 letter Dickinson poetically recalls an incident in which an Indian woman had come to her kitchen door "with gay Baskets and a dazzling Baby" (L 653). About her conversation with the Indian woman, Dickinson writes:

> Her little Boy "once died," she said, Death to her dispelling him—I asked what the Baby liked, and she said "to step." The Prairie before the Door was gay with Flowers of Hay, and I led her in—She argued with the Birds—she leaned on Clover Walls and they fell, and dropped her—With jargon sweeter than a Bell, she grappled Buttercups—and they sank together, the Buttercups the heaviest— What sweetest use of Days!

The first reference in the letter of 1879 documents Dickinson's knowledge of the prairie's significance to American literature at the time, Mary Higginson's book being a collection of essays. The reference in the letter of 1880, furthermore, documents Dickinson's understanding of conventional poetic use of prairie imagery. In diction, tone, and imaginative association the letter's first paragraph, quoted above, seems closer to poetry than to prose. To be called poetry by nineteenth-century standards the paragraph needs only to be arranged in stanza form: the rhythms are already nearly those of Dickinson's usual hymnal measure. The prairie is associated here with Indians, flowers, and birds, three recurrent images in prairie poetry. The odd reference to the boy who "once died" connects the prairie to eternity and the spiritual realm. The baby liking "to step" suggests the nomadic life of the Indian on the prairie and the close relationship between the prairie and the humans dwelling on it. Because the Indian woman is living at the whim and from the charity of the white race, not on the prairie with which Dickinson associates her, Dickinson also implies the theme of the displacement of the Native Americans.

In two poems Dickinson refers to the prairies specifically—"To make a prairie" and "My period had come for Prayer—" (P 564). In the latter poem Dickinson draws on images and themes of the prairie metaphor that she shares with many other nineteenth-century poets. She equates the prairies with air, and therefore the heavens, and further suggests the metaphysical significance of the prairies by reference to prayer and worship. She also employs the themes of settling the American frontier, of limitlessness, of solitude. She uses the images of silence and of the horizon continually receding in front of the traveler. The poem reads:

> My period had come for Prayer—
> No other Art—would do—
> My Tactics missed a rudiment—
> Creator—Was it you?
>
> God grows above—so those who pray
> Horizons—must ascend—

And so I stepped upon the North
To see this Curious Friend—

His House was not—no sign had He—
By Chimney—nor by Door
Could I infer his Residence—
Vast Prairies of Air

Unbroken by a Settler—
Were all that I could see—
Infinitude—Had'st Thou no Face
That I might look on Thee?

The Silence condescended—
Creation stopped—for Me—
But awed beyond my errand—
I worshipped—did not "pray"—

Besides sharing these conventional themes, Dickinson also makes a unique metaphorical use of the prairies. Creating an extended metaphor of prairie settlement in the last half of the poem, she places God in this figurative, spiritual frontier. As the horizon on the actual prairies continually recedes in front of the settlers moving westward, so does the spiritual horizon continually move away from the petitioner to God: "so those who pray / Horizons— must ascend." Like the settlers, the speaker, while she ascends these horizons to reach God's "Residence," can see only "Vast prairies of Air / Unbroken by a Settler—." These prairies are also "Infinitude" in "Silence." The speaker, upon reaching this spiritual height, "worshipped—did not 'pray'—" The prairies, then, not only represent limitlessness and the spiritual realm; they also represent one's intensely individual and private adoration of God.[8]

Because many images and themes developed by Dickinson in her poems about the plains and prairies are conventional, she was obviously aware of this American metaphor and its use in the poetry of her day.[9] "My period had come for Prayer—" reveals her use of conventional themes along with her use of unconventional form and unique metaphoric associations. The dashes, the capital letters, and the slant rhymes in stanzas 3 and 5 are characteristic of her prosodic "eccentricities." The ambiguous syntax in stanza 3 (line 2 being simultaneously the ending of one sentence and the beginning of another) and the disturbed rhythm in the line "Vast Prairies of Air," through their unconventionality, call particular attention to the prairie imagery. That imagery is associatively and uniquely connected with art, prairie settlement, and God and prayer.

"To make a prairie" is almost entirely unconventional in theme, form, and imagery. Its primary theme is the power of the creative, poetic imagination. It employs no standard stanza, various line lengths, one very short line, and very quick rhymes. While the poem's chief images of the prairie—clover and bee—also serve other nineteenth-century poets as common images of the prairie, those other poets rely on more images, including the sun, various types of wildlife, grass, rivers, the horizon, and open space. Dickinson's prairie, on the other hand, consists only of "revery." Not only is the imagery of "To make a prairie" unconventional because of its lack of variety; it is also extreme in its denial of the need to use specific prairie images in order to create a poetic prairie.

Its imagery is unconventional in yet another significant way. While most popular nineteenth-century poets depict the prairie as a fertile place, they avoid the sexual implications of birds, bees, and flowers. Dickinson, however, reinforces the sexual imagery in her poem by concentrating only on the clover and the bee.[10] The bee will light on, or enter, the clover—an act suggestive of a sexual encounter because these two, together, can "make a prairie." Yet, the imagination alone can make the prairie if the male bee is absent. Dickinson, in a dual poetic act very unlike her contemporaries', first stresses the sexual aspect of the prairie's fertility, then contradicts the common, societal reaction to such an extremely unconventional reference to sex. She subverts the procreative quality of the sex act by denying the necessity of the male sexual partner.

For Melville the prairie is nightmarish. In his prairie poetry the creative power of the individual poet thrives weedlike in the

American garden. In *Clarel* (1876) and *John Marr and Other Sailors* (1888), Melville echoes the conventional, nationalistic themes associated with the prairies, but he subverts their significance and uses them to emphasize the isolation of the artist in a democracy. For Clarel and John Marr, and for Melville, the prairies are a place of unactualized hopes and failed ideals—a place that in actuality belies the American dream, a place that in the imagination is haunted only by specters of the past.

Clarel, a "young divinity student tormented by doubts,"[11] is touring the Holy Land on a quest for spiritual rebirth. On his pilgrimage he questions his Christian faith, which has been upset by forces of Deism and Darwinism. Stanley Brodwin lists the turmoil of forces that affect Clarel: "isolation and alienation, the failure of reason, the agonized freedom to choose from among a welter of conflicting and paradoxical faiths, the death of God, and above all, death's stamp of limitation on man."[12]

The tragic plot emphasizes Clarel's doubt and the accompanying desolation. While in Jerusalem, Clarel falls in love with Ruth, a young Jewish girl. Ruth's father is killed by Arabs, and according to Jewish custom, Clarel cannot see Ruth during her period of mourning. Clarel grieves because of the separation, and he travels the Holy Land to comfort himself. When he returns to Jerusalem, he finds that Ruth has died of grief. Not only is Clarel left bearing the grief of his loss, but he bears the guilt of not having been able to comfort Ruth in her grief. The narrator enjoins Clarel in the epilogue to "Keep thy heart": "Emerge thou mayst from the last whelming sea, / And prove that death but routs life into victory."[13] But at the end of the story "Clarel's future seems more uncertain than ever."[14]

This plot is the background of Clarel's spiritual quest. Both *A Poem and a Pilgrimage,* as Melville states in the subtitle, the work is chiefly an account of Clarel's spiritual questioning, searching, and desolation.[15] The opening of the poem introduces Clarel's desolation through the irony of Jerusalem's appearance. Rather than seeing the mythically divine city of Jerusalem, Clarel sees upon his arrival,

at the last, aloft for goal,
Like the ice-bastions round the Pole,
Thy blank, blank towers, Jerusalem! (4)

This irony is enforced by a reference to the prairie about twenty lines before this first description of Jerusalem. The group Clarel is traveling with has crossed a "plain" on the way to the city:

The plain we crossed. In afternoon,
How like our early autumn bland—
So softly tempered for a boon—
The breath of Sharon's prairie land! (4)

On this prairie of hope, as they near the divine city, the group sees the optimistic symbol, the rose of Sharon. The appearance of the city, however, subverts the idea of hope and portends the tragedy of the story.

Melville's poem is not merely a story of Clarel's spiritual predicament. As the subtitle suggests, the poem is also a pilgrimage, for the narrator, Clarel, author, and reader: for author because the poem is the result of Melville's actual journey to the Holy Land, for reader because of his or her discoveries about the spiritual state of the reader's contemporary world made by engaging with Clarel's pilgrimage and realizations and with Melville's images and symbols. Because the Old World of Jerusalem is a type of the New World in the poem, Jerusalem's degenerate state is representative of the world's spiritual state. As Lawrence Buell writes, "*Clarel's* presumption concerning the national project—not the American alone but all forms of modern nationalism—seems to be that the riddle of identity, in all the ways that term can be construed, leads back to the ancient world, which supplies a venue for examining the wreckage of latter-day Levantine and Euro-American civilization as interchangeable symptoms of the bankruptcy of nineteenth-century thought."[16] This "bankruptcy" or degeneracy is the central discovery of the narrator, Clarel, author, and reader on the pilgrimage.

The theme of a failed New World builds in the poem until

the narrator explicitly voices it ("they" in this passage refers to Clarel and his companions):

> They felt how far beyond the scope
> Of elder Europe's saddest thought
> Might be the New World's sudden brought
> In youth to share old age's pains—
> To feel the arrest of hope's advance,
> And squandered last inheritance;
> And cry—"To Terminus build fanes!
> Columbus ended earth's romance:
> No New World to mankind remains!" (484)

Melville places Clarel in the ancient land to show how the hope of America has failed: an American must return to the distant past to try to find meaning and faith since there is none for him in America. Robert Milder suggests that Melville's shift to this attitude can be identified by a comparison between *Battle-Pieces and Aspects of the War* (1866) and *Clarel* (1876). *Battle-Pieces* "sets itself the task of re-creating the 'good American' according to a pattern that promises spiritual redemption to the nation [after the Civil War] and vocational redemption to Melville, its neglected man of letters" (174). But, Milder asserts, Melville's hopes for redeeming America "were defeated by the course of Reconstruction and the critical indifference to *Battle-Pieces*" so that in *Clarel* he "despair[ed] of its fulfillment in any modern nation."[17]

Because it is especially leveled at Jerusalem, the ancient world, and at America, the New World and the beacon of hope for the world at large, the irony of Jerusalem's appearance posits the denigrated spiritual state of all mankind. As I have pointed out, Melville also suggests the equation of a failed world and a failed America in his reference to "Sharon's prairie land." The story of Nathan, an episode within the larger narrative of *Clarel*, binds firmer the images of the prairies with America and mankind's spiritual failing.

Nathan's familial roots are in the American pilgrims who

were "austere, ascetical, but free" (57). Those settlers, over genera-
tions, pushed west to the Illinois prairies, where Nathan's father
came with his family. The prairies are juxtaposed, at first, to the
"gloom . . . of grim hemlock woods / Breeding the witchcraft-spell
malign" (57–58). The prairies contain the conventionally opposite
connotations:

> But who the gracious charm may tell—
> Long rollings of the vast serene—
> The prairie in her swimming swell
> Of undulation. (58)

The Illinois prairies are, in fact, "a turf divine / Of promise, how
auspicious spread" (58). In such a promised land Nathan grows up
in the faith of his fathers.

"After some years," however, things begin to change (58).
Like Clarel, Nathan begins to doubt his Christian faith:

> The sway
> He felt of his grave life, and power
> Of vast space, from the log-house door
> Daily beheld. (58)

The vastness of the prairies no longer suggests serenity and divinity,
but to Nathan it represents emptiness and death, as the pun on
*grave* suggests. Three Indian burial mounds in sight of Nathan's
farm emphasize the thoughts of death and the encroaching dark-
ness in his soul as they cast a shadow on the infinity of the prairies.
By likening the Egyptian pyramids to the burial mounds, Melville
suggests the likeness of Nathan's and Clarel's spiritual dilemmas and
further asserts the similarity between the New World's and the
Ancient World's spiritual decay.

Further clear signs of the world's spiritual decay appear to
Nathan on the prairies. The three Indian burial mounds represent a
physical death that cannot become a spiritual rebirth: the Indians
and Egyptians, after all, are pagans with whom Melville ironically

associates the Holy Trinity (in the three mounds). The prairies around the mounds contain even more graphic images of death and decay for Nathan:

> Hard by, as chanced, he once beheld
> Bones like sea corals; one bleached skull
> A vase vined round and beautiful
> With flowers; felt, with bated breath
> The floral revelry over death. (59)

Both the sea and flowers, two symbols of life and two common images of the prairies, are associated with death here—a relentless, bleaching death. We know that Nathan misunderstands the flowers' "revelry over death" because of the flowers' transitory and delicate life as compared to the permanence of death, which is represented by the skull vase. To make certain that we recognize Nathan's mistake, Melville reveals the other images of the prairies that both shape and reflect Nathan's spiritual character:

> And other sights his heart had thrilled;
> Lambs had he known by thunder killed,
> Innocents—and the type of Christ
> Betrayed. (59)

The prairie becomes a metaphor for man's corruption: on it Christ's "type" is not merely "killed," but "betrayed." There is no hope of resurrection.

As the physical prairies reflect America's and mankind's spiritual decay, they also induce imaginative experiences that are equally revealing. "In prairie twilight," the sunset that conventionally invokes thoughts of beauty and glory, Nathan has a waking dream of the death of his uncle, who was buried beneath a rock slide in the White Mountains. "These thoughts unhinged him," and chancing upon a copy of Thomas Paine's *The Age of Reason*, Nathan falls further (59). He discards his Christianity for the "Deist sway," the "Pantheistic sway" (61). That sway,

Broad as the prairie fire, consumed
Some pansies which before had bloomed
Within his heart; it did but feed
To clear the soil for upstart weed. (61)

The equation is clear: Nathan's spiritual decay is America's spiritual decay.[18]

Unable to relieve his spiritual disease with Deism, Nathan continues his spiritual quest. He meets a Jewish maiden, Agar, with whom he falls deeply in love. Converting to Judaism, he marries Agar. Later, he and his family emigrate to "Sharon's plain" because Nathan, with some "zealous Jews," wants to "reinstate the Holy Land" (64). His situation is again similar to Clarel's: "Backward still the inquirer goes / To get behind man's present lot / Of crumbling faith" (63). Nathan becomes so obsessed with his cause that Agar tries to dissuade him, but he will not sway this time. Not even his infant son's death turns his "inveterate zeal" (66). The narrator of this story tells Clarel that Nathan "was modified" in time (66), but at the cost of the loss of his son and the loss of Agar's love. Nathan's leaving America, becoming an apostate from its ideals of the future, and searching the past of another land for spiritual rebirth mirrors Clarel's quest: Nathan does not find his spiritual ease in the Holy Land, nor does Clarel. Melville's equation is now complete: Nathan's spiritual decay is Clarel's, is America's, is the world's.

Nathan's story is told by Nehemiah, "a millenarian and irrepressible dispenser of tracts,"[19] whom Clarel accepts in part as a spiritual guide. Nehemiah has left America and journeyed to the Holy Land for the Second Coming. His telling the story, then, adds another level of irony: the optimist recounts a story of faith lost and not regained. Nehemiah weakly ends his story of Nathan, "Events will speak" (66), an ending that parallels the ending of *Clarel*, for Clarel is also finally left in a spiritual and emotional limbo. Nathan's story is Clarel's story, an equation that points to the strongest irony: the girl with whom Clarel falls in love is Ruth, Nathan's daughter.

Both Nathan's story and Clarel's story defame America as the land of hope and promise. The prairies are an integral part of

Nathan's experience: they are important to the genesis of his story and to the genesis and shaping of its main character. Melville inverts the conventional significance of the prairies, however, to enforce his ironic perspective. Their vastness, flowers, similarity to the sea, and Indian mounds do not attest to their glorious infinity, beauty, majesty, nor timelessness. Rather, these images represent emptiness and death without chance of resurrection, thus reinforcing the spiritual sterility of America. The American dream of hope and promise has become, not Dickinson's "revery," but a waking nightmare of a rock slide down the White Mountains.[20] The prairies also represent the spiritual decay of the world, an ironic inversion of Whitman's placing of the prairies at the heart of America, which is in turn at the heart of the world. Compared to the representative poems of the optimistic metaphor, *Clarel* is indeed an "upstart weed" in the American garden.

Clarel's quest is a personal one for spiritual fulfillment, and Melville's depiction of the prairie metaphor is a personal rendering that derogates the conventional optimistic metaphor. Melville's publishing experiences indicate that, like Dickinson, he also became a private poet—although Melville, who published four books of poetry, was in a sense more persistent. The 1866 publication by Harper's of twelve hundred copies of *Battle-Pieces and Aspects of the War* resulted, not in failure, but not in success either. *Clarel* was completely neglected, and Melville published only twenty-five copies each of *John Marr and Other Sailors* (1888) and *Timoleon* (1891), intending to give them only to his friends. What Wai-chee Dimock claims about Melville's fiction is also obviously true about his poetry, "Authorship, for him, is almost exclusively an exercise in freedom, an attempt to proclaim the self's sovereignty over and against the world's."[21]

By publishing only twenty-five copies each of his last two books of poetry, Melville publicly acknowledged that his poetry was not for a popular audience.[22] His shift to that attitude is further documented in some references to prairies in minor poems. A very conventional prairie poem comes of his visit to Illinois in 1840: "Trophies of Peace" celebrates the "termless yield" of "files on files of Prairie Maize."[23] In "Donelson," one of the *Battle-Pieces*, Melville writes that the Union troops march toward Donelson *"full of* vim *from Western prairies won"* (18, Melville's emphasis). This statement is Whitmanesque in its characterization of the prairies as representative of the Union's might and character, and even though Melville makes an antiwar poem of "Donelson," this reference to the prairies does not have the strong ironic import that the prairie references do in *Clarel*. Later, in *Timoleon*, one prairie reference appears in "After the Pleasure Party," in which the speaker's passions sweep her soul "Like prairie fires that spurn control / Where withering *weeds* incense the flame" (217, my emphasis). The poem is a dramatic monologue, the speaker being a woman "who has devoted her years of youth to scholarly and intellectual pursuits, denying the sensual pleasures, only to find that love will not be gainsaid, that the scorn of love has brought its own revenge in unfulfillment."[24] The early, conventionally optimistic allusions to the prairies are drastically changed to connote self-consuming, personally denigrating emotional vapidity.

*John Marr* emphasizes Melville's shift in attitude as well. While Melville uses the theme of the isolated self in *John Marr*, a theme that also runs through *Clarel*, he uses it in a different way. Whereas *Clarel* centers mainly on a cultural and spiritual dilemma, *John Marr* centers primarily on a cultural and social one—the dilemma of one's isolation from people of the same cast of mind. The two works do meet, however, at a cultural point. In both works America is responsible for the alienation of the individual. The metaphor of the prairie has shown this in *Clarel*, and the same metaphor reveals it in *John Marr*. John Marr, a retired sailor, is marooned on the western prairies. With this irony Melville adds another dimension to his prairie metaphor. As John Marr becomes increasingly isolated on the prairies, he imaginatively communes with his old shipmates. Thus John Marr's imaginative conversations, because they are parallel with Melville's "imaginative" conversations—his poetry printed only for friends, become a comment on the artistic isolation of the poet who is not a *popular poet* in nineteenth-century America.

*John Marr* begins with a lengthy prose introduction that characterizes his and Melville's view of the prairies. Moving west in 1838 to a "frontier-prairie," John Marr marries, only to lose his wife and child to the fever. They are buried in one coffin, their grave being "another mound, . . . in the wide prairie," not far from the larger Indian mounds. The mother and child become, along with the Indians in their mounds, "one common clay, under a strange terrace serpentine in form" (159). With the image of the snake intruding on a would-be Eden, this introduction to the prairies, like Nathan's final view of the prairies, ironically stresses sterility and death.

John Marr will not leave the prairies that hold his loved ones, and though the pain of his loss lessens, "the void at heart remains" (160). He attempts to socialize with the settlers on the prairies but cannot because they do not share the same past, and Melville would have it, contrary to Whitman's futurist concept of America and the prairies, that "one cannot always be talking about the present, much less speculating about the future" (160). So John Marr is isolated, chiefly because of the limits of the settlers, whose "mental reach" was "so limited unavoidably" that the ocean to them was "but a hearsay" (160). These people are limited in other ways, too: they are "staid"; "ascetic"; morally biased; "sincerely, however, narrowly, religious"; and lacking "geniality, the flower of life" (160–61). Most importantly, they are separate from, not closer to, nature. And this separation is, ironically and unconventionally, reflective of nature's own indifference. The settlers are "standing . . . next of kin to Nature," yet their "unresponsiveness" to their "fellow-creatures . . . seemed of a piece with the apathy of Nature herself as envisaged to him here on a prairie where none but the perished mound-builders had as yet left a durable mark" (161).

The conventional prairie images used to characterize the people of the prairies are again ironically inverted by Melville. The prairie's vastness complements Marr's emptiness of heart, as it emphasizes his isolation. The settlers on the prairies demonstrate, not hope for the future, but a constriction by the past. Not only are the prairies temporally limited, but they are imaginatively limited as well, since the settlers' "mental reach" is so constrained that they cannot even fully appreciate their memories of the ocean. Melville thus belittles an image that is often used to describe and give metaphorical depth to the prairies. Finally, the flower image is debunked: instead of being profuse, the "flower" of geniality is the chief want of the settlers. Melville's depiction of the prairie settlers discharges the whole idea that the prairie frontier brings one closer to humanity because it brings one closer to nature.

Using the theme of the destruction of the wilderness, Melville continues to denigrate America by emphasizing the human distance from nature on the prairies. Both the native human population and the animal population have been forced from the prairies by the encroachment of "municipalities and States." America, therefore, has been the downfall of these men and beasts, and America has made the "plain a desert," which is "forsaken" and sterile, rather than fertile. The prairie's vastness stresses its lifelessness, as does the familiar image of the ocean: the prairie is the "bed of a dried-up sea" (162). Summarizing America's responsibility for this devastation, Melville writes that the prairies attest to

> yet another successive overleaped limit of civilized life; a life which in America can to-day hardly be said to have any western bound but the ocean that washes Asia. Throughout these plains, now in places overpopulous with towns overopulent; sweeping plains, elsewhere fenced off in every direction into flourishing farms—pale townsmen and hale farmers alike, in part, the descendants of the first sallow settlers; . . . of this prairie, now everywhere intersected with wire and rail, hardly can it be said that at the period here written of there was so much as a traceable road. (163)

Again, the familiar theme of limitlessness and the Whitmanesque theme of America being the bridge between the Old World and the New World are ironically inverted. The hope that the prairies should represent is bypassed, overridden.

Briefly Melville invokes the conventional theme of the prairie's abundance: the "region that half a century ago produced little for the sustenance of man, . . . today launch[es] its superabundant wheat-harvest on the world" (163). But this reference is enclosed within the diatribe against overpopulation and overopulence, and it stands alone amid a number of negative statements about the prairies. The "superabundance," therefore, represents America's overopulence, which makes America imperialistic and destructive.

After making this ironic inversion, Melville returns to the image of the sea, which is, after all, appropriate to John Marr, but again Melville redoubles his irony. To John Marr the prairies are like the ocean only in their loneliness: to the prairie's "denizen, a friend left behind anywhere in the world seemed not alone absent to sight, but an absentee from existence" (164). His friends absent from existence as far as he is concerned, John Marr resorts to his imagination and holds "verbal communion" with his old shipmates. Doing so, he populates the prairies with their ghosts. The prairies pull Marr deeper and deeper into this imaginative life, which creates only "phantoms of the dead" (164): "as the growing sense of his environment threw him more and more upon retrospective musings, these phantoms, next to those of his wife and child, became spiritual companions" (164).

John Marr, then, is completely removed from a material world, and since his isolation is that of an "imaginative heart," it represents the isolation of the artist who uses words to communicate with an audience. Figuratively, Melville's audience is dead. Like John Marr's neighbors on the prairies, Melville's living audience, according to Melville, does not have enough people in it with sufficiently imaginative minds to support him. Deriding the conventional themes and images of the American prairies, Melville uses his version of the prairie metaphor to show that America is to blame for the rejection of its artists.

Furthermore, at the end of the introductory prose section of *John Marr*, Marr speaks in verse to his old shipmates. Because his address is a poem, it suggests that his solitude is the isolation of the literary artist. The structure of the lyrical sequence in *John Marr* also reinforces both Marr's and Melville's distances from their audiences. The poems of *John Marr and Other Sailors* can all be viewed as John Marr's imaginative conversations with his shipmates. The first lyric, "John Marr," is an introduction to the narrative voice of the poetic sequence. The second poem, "Bridegroom Dick," is a reply to John Marr. It introduces another point of view, since it is spoken by Dick, and it introduces other sailors, as Dick recounts some old sea stories. The third lyric, a much shorter one, is from the point of view of Tom Deadlight, who is dying of fever and losing his grip on reality. "Jack Roy" is a lyric about a heroic and jovial sailor.

These imaginative communications with old sailors then open up to the subgroups "Sea-Pieces," "Minor Sea-Pieces," and "Pebbles." It is possible that John Marr is still speaking these poems: they show him becoming imaginatively further and further removed from his actual existence on the prairie as his lyrics become more private and meditative. At the end of the prose introduction to "John Marr" Melville suggests this regression deeper and deeper into the imagination. He writes that John Marr "invokes" the "visionary ones," the imaginative phantoms of his sailing days, "striving, as it were, to get into verbal communion with them, or, under yet stronger illusion, reproaching them for their silence" (164). Because the "visionary ones" speak in poems, Melville forcefully links the imagination with poetry.

The lyrics of "Sea-Pieces" and the later sections evolve from being character descriptions of sailors projected from their own and others' points of view to meditations on the sea and fate. A poem about a ship that was wrecked twice, each time after being followed portentously by three albatross-like birds, "The Haglets" questions the imminent doom of the ship. "The Maldive Shark" questions the reason for the existence of the "jaws of the Fates" (200), and "The Berg" is a meditation on the seemingly fated collision of a ship and an iceberg. Most of the poems in this sequence of the book deal with such gloomy subjects, with only two exceptions ("Jack Roy" and "To Ned"). Such subjects, particularly fate, are certainly appropriate to John Marr, who is fated to live out his life on the prairies and whose wife and child were fated to die on the prairies.

The structure of the book reveals not only Marr's isolation but also Melville's artistic isolation. The predominantly grim subject matter of the poems and the movement that I have outlined above, from the narrative "Bridegroom Dick" to the meditative poems later in the sequence, show Marr's and Melville's delving into the self for the subject matter of the poems.[25] Furthermore, the seven "Pebbles" at the end of the book illustrate the very private and meditative quality that the book ultimately achieves.

First, it is not clear whether "Pebbles" is one poem or seven. If they constitute one poem, none of the seven stanzas is in the same form as any other, and only two are even the same length. If, on the other hand, they are seven separate poems, they do form a sequence. This structural ambiguity highlights the extremely imaginative quality of the end of the book.

Second, though each stanza is numbered, as if together they compose a sequence, their connections to one another are highly associative and intuitive rather than logical—as if they express the movement of a private mind rather than attempt any type of communication. The surface structure of the sequence consists of a movement from land to sea to the metaphysical: part 1 is about the "winds" that "blow whither they list"; part 2 moves "to the beaches," part 3 to the "liquid hills," part 4 to "the ocean," and part 6 to "Christ." The associative, thematic structure moves from "winds" that "blow whither they list" (part 1); to "Truth" (part 2); to "the dream in [man's] brain" (part 3); to "Man, suffering inflictor" (part 4); to "the old implacable Sea" (part 5); to "the Dragon's heaven-challenging crest" and "Christ on the Mount, and the dove in her nest" (part 6); and to a speaker who is "Healed of my hurt" (part 7)—all associations with an individual's spiritual crisis.

Third, the speaking voice in "Pebbles" shifts, and not as conventionally as in the first poems of *John Marr*, where each complete poem is spoken by a single voice. The voice of the first four parts speaks aphoristically, the only hint of doubt being two rhetorical questions in part 2. In part 5, by contrast, the sea itself speaks:

"Implacable I, the old implacable Sea." Part 6 is then spoken by another voice, presumably by the speaker of parts 1–4, assuredly not by the sea. In part 6, however, the speaker is no longer so self-assured as he ponders the supreme power of God:

> Curled in the comb of yon billow Andean,
>> Is it the Dragon's heaven-challenging crest?
> Elemental mad ramping of ravening waters—
>> Yet Christ on the Mount, and the dove in her
>> nest! (206)

The question mark reveals the speaker's uncertainty, and the question is never answered. Only the juxtaposition of the "mad ramping of ravening waters" with the images of Christ and the dove remain, as if no logical answer is possible. Part 7 states that a personal faith is the only possible answer. The speaker of part 7 (the same as parts 1–4 and 6) has apparently passed his spiritual crisis, and he celebrates the sea, which helped him:

> Healed of my Hurt, I laud the inhuman Sea—
> Yea, bless the Angels Four that there convene;
> For healed I am even by their pitiless breath
> Distilled in wholesome dew named rosmarine. (206)

Melville clearly delineates the inquiring and ambivalent character of the lyrical "I," of the human speaker in "Pebbles."[26] The lyrical sequence of the book, therefore, depicts the isolation of both Marr and Melville as the structure continually loosens until in "Pebbles" it is almost purely associative.

Through John Marr, Melville portrays the isolation of the poet in nineteenth-century America, and through Clarel, he depicts the spiritual deterioration of America and the world. The prairie metaphor is at the figurative heart of Melville's poetic display.

The two private, poetic voices of Emily Dickinson and Herman Melville counter the popular voices of nineteenth-century prairie poetry. Rather than laud the hope of a democratic America, these voices lament the threat that a mass culture imposes on the individual artist.

In her poems about the prairies, Dickinson emphasizes the imaginative capacity of the artist, not the national achievements of democratic America. Her prairie metaphor thus represents the creative power of the individual poet and implies that the prairies do not innately contain, as the popular poets would have it, the essence of America. Rather, her treatment of that geography is perceptualist—the prairies signify what the poet makes them signify. Her short poem "To make a prairie," for example, succinctly states that the prairie is mostly open space, which acquires its significance from the imagination of the artist—from "revery."

Dickinson has easily, even flippantly (if we read the light tone of "To make a prairie" as sarcasm), revealed the limits of the metaphor, showing that the artist can make of it what she or he wishes. In so doing she has set herself apart from the mainstream of nineteenth-century American poetry. Writing for a common, democratic audience would constrain her poetic imagination and, ironically, her artistic freedom.

For Melville the conventional metaphor has become a nightmare. Like Dickinson, he remakes it in order to reveal its limits. But more extreme than Dickinson, he uses it to accuse America of denigrating and isolating its poets, and he ironically inverts the metaphor to suggest not only that too conventional and too simplistic a view of America demonstrates a misunderstanding of what America is, but also that such a misunderstanding contributes to America's spiritual and artistic decline.

# CHAPTER FIVE

# REAPING THE HARVEST
## The Expanse of the Metaphor
## in the Combining Voice
## of Walt Whitman

Whereas Melville berates the popular themes of democracy and holds America responsible for denying a place to the private poet, Walt Whitman loudly sounds democratic themes and combines them with the theme of the *self*. Reflecting the nationalistic optimism of the popular poets, Whitman's prairies represent America, which in turn represents a future ideal. On the other hand, this new landscape of America, he proclaims, offers the opportunity for full realization of the self. Developing both nationalistic and private themes in his prairie metaphor, Whitman speaks, furthermore, in both public and private voices—singing "one's self," yet uttering "the word En-Masse." On the one hand, his very personal associations and revelations are spoken in a private voice. His theorizing about a national literature and his pluralistic language, on the other hand, demonstrate his desire to create a public voice. As Betsy Erkkila demonstrates, Whitman's language is part of a "national debate about the relationship between language and culture in America," and his "foreign borrowings," particularly French terms, are an "effort to create a . . . racially and ethnically mixed language to match America's democratic pluralism."[1] Combining public and private themes and voices, Whitman reaps the harvest of the prairie metaphor.

*Leaves of Grass* is Whitman's poetic geography of the United

States. The "constituting metaphor," to use Edwin Fussell's term, of the poet's lifelong work is *grass*.[2] The prairies and plains, whose main characteristic is grass, also become metaphorically central to Whitman's prose and poetry. They constitute both the geographical and figurative heart of America as well as the structural and figurative center of *Specimen Days* and *Leaves of Grass*. They are, according to Whitman in *Specimen Days*, "America's Characteristic Landscape."[3] Furthermore, Whitman's prose explicitly acknowledges the metaphorical importance of the prairies, identifying the prairies as a fitting background for the greatest work of American literature and boldly stating that the prairies are the most appropriate image of the new democratic country. America is, in turn, the future of the world. Throughout Whitman, the democratic light of America illumines the future, carrying the torch of freedom, equality, unity, and hope to the rest of the world. Again, the prairies and plains are central to this concept, for Whitman calls America in "Starting from Paumanok" the "land of the pastoral plains, the grass-fields of the world."[4] In his poetry, he places the prairies and plains in key positions, both in citations of geographical areas of the United States and within the "geography," or structure, of individual poems.

Always, in both prose and poetry, the prairies reflect the metaphorical significance of the "grass" cited in the title of his ongoing, single poetic creation. They are common and democratic. They are material. They are spiritual. Their leaves, or blades, are individual. As the "journey-work of the stars," they represent America in its cosmic proportions. Throughout Whitman's works, images of the prairies represent these essential American themes and others, such as, abundance, diversity, future, progress, hope, equality, liberty, and unity.

Unlike Melville's private voice, therefore, Whitman's voice celebrates the significance of America and the prairies, for the American poet as well as for Americans in general and for the world. Like the voices of the public poets, Whitman's voice celebrates, reveres, the New World as the place to realize the spiritual potential of human existence. Democratic America thus becomes, in Whitman's prairie metaphor, a material incarnation of a spiritual ideal. The prairies and plains in Whitman's poetry thus not only represent the themes of American democracy and unite the public with the private voice, but also, by explicitly associating the prairies with the cosmos, signify most completely the union of the physical and metaphysical.

## "AMERICA'S CHARACTERISTIC LANDSCAPE"
### The Prairies in Whitman's Prose

When Whitman calls the plains and prairies of central North America "America's Characteristic Landscape" in *Specimen Days*, he imbues the area with themes of American democracy. These include the familiar and popular roots, stems, and leaves of democracy: freedom, equality, "America's Bulk Average" (*Prose* 2:706–7), and diversity being unified. Whitman adds to these nationalistic notions the universal themes of life's cyclical regeneration, the equality of life and death, and the transcendence of the material into the spiritual. Furthermore, in *Specimen Days* he particularly associates the plains and prairies with a national literature. For Whitman, then, this landscape becomes the literary symbol of democratic America's potential—the incarnation of human perfection, the realization of the ideal.

Whitman's prose stresses the early and continued importance of the prairies and plains to poetry and to a national political identity. In the 1855 preface to *Leaves of Grass* he associates the American bard with, among other geographical regions, the prairies. The spirit of the American poet, he writes, "responds to his country's spirit . . . . he incarnates its geography," which includes "pasturage sweet and free as savanah or upland or prairie" (*LG* 713; Whitman's ellipsis). In 1856, in his impassioned plea for the Union, *The Eighteenth Presidency!*, Whitman calls the prairies the "real West," from where, he implies, the "Delegates of the Politicians" should come.[5] "Democratic Vistas" (1870) announces, "In a few years the dominion-heart of America will be far inland, toward the West." It is "likely" that "our future national capitol . . . will migrate a thousand or two miles" (*Prose* 2:384–85).

In *Specimen Days* (1882) Whitman published his view of

middle America, recording his responses to his trip to the Rocky Mountains. While this "Long Jaunt West" lasted from September to December 1879, the actual time Whitman spent on the prairies and plains was about two weeks at the end of September and the beginning of October. "The Prairies" is the copy of a speech he intended to deliver, but did not (most likely because of illness), at the Kansas State Silver Wedding in Bismarck Grove, Kansas.[6] In it Whitman reaffirms the symbolic role of the prairies. The brief speech ends with an encapsulating statement. After acknowledging that all other geographical areas of the United States "are equally and integrally and indissolubly this Nation," he says of the prairies: "But this favor'd central area of (in round numbers) two thousand miles square seems fated to be the home both of what I would call America's distinctive ideas and distinctive realities" (*Prose* 1:208). The prairies are America's "central area," literally and figuratively, geographically and ideally. They embody the major themes of the new democracy, and they contain and impart the character of the men that live on them.

Of course, the occasion and audience would in part have dictated the tone of Whitman's comments, but later sections of *Specimen Days* reiterate his exuberance. The prairies provide goods for the rest of the country: the "plain and prairie area . . . is the inexhaustible land of wheat, maize, wool, flax, coal, iron, beef and pork, butter and cheese, apples and grapes—land of ten million virgin farms." Furthermore, America and its prairies serve a significant role in world history. The bounty of the plains and prairies is not only for America, which is the light of the world's future, but also for the entire world, for "upon [the plains] . . . may easily be grown enough wheat to feed the world" (*Prose* 1:220).

*Specimen Days* also emphasizes the aesthetic capacity of the prairies. Comparing them to mountain scenery, he writes that the "Prairies and Plains, while less stunning at first sight, last longer, fill the esthetic sense fuller, precede all the rest, and make North America's characteristic landscape." He continues, reiterating what he intended to speak at Bismarck Grove: "Indeed through the whole of this journey, with all its shows and varieties, what most impress'd me, and will longest remain with me, are these same prairies. Day after day, and night after night, to my eyes, to all my senses—the esthetic one most of all—they silently and broadly unfolded. Even their simplest statistics are sublime" (*Prose* 1:221). Because the place and the themes associated with it are particularly American for Whitman, the joining of the prairies with the aesthetic sensibility establishes the prairies as the dominating American metaphor.

While he goes on to proclaim the role of this metaphor in American literature in general, more specific to his own literary inclinations is the section of *Specimen Days* Whitman titles "The Prairies and Great Plains in Poetry." He proclaims the unifying tendency of democracy and the prairies' metaphorical association with that tendency:

> Grand as the thought that doubtless the child is already born who will see a hundred millions of people, the most prosperous and advanc'd of the world, inhabiting these Prairies, the great Plains, and the valley of the Mississippi, I could not help thinking it would be grander still to see all those inimitable American areas fused in the alembic of a perfect poem, or other esthetic work, entirely western, fresh and limitless—altogether our own, without a trace or taste of Europe's soil, reminiscence, technical letter or spirit. (*Prose* 1:219)

He continues this entry, which suggests progress and prosperity, with a list of other themes and images that stress the "sense of vastness" of the prairies. There are "characteristic" visions of "the cactuses, pinks, buffalo grass, wild sage," "prairie-dogs and . . . herds of antelope." There is the association of the land with the sky in "the receding perspective, and the far circle-line of the horizon" that continually expresses the limitlessness of the prairies and the connection between the physical and the metaphysical. "The clear, pure, cool, rarefied nutriment for the lungs, previously quite unknown" emphasizes how the spiritual essence of the prairies incorporates itself in the human inhabitants.

The metaphor of the prairies in Whitman's prose follows the trend he describes in the preface to the 1855 edition of *Leaves of Grass* and in "Democratic Vistas." That trend is from an incipient democracy to a human divinity, and the poet will lead the way to this paradise on earth. In the preface the poet will, priestlike, lead the people of the democracy to "a new order" in which "every man shall be his own priest" (*Prose* 2:456). In "Democratic Vistas" Whitman looks into the future to announce, "The Priest departs, the divine literatus comes" (*Prose* 2:365). The prairies represent, for Whitman, the many themes of America—its vastness, ambiguity, freedom, equality, democracy, and diversity becoming unified. That is, the prairies symbolize the future, ideal potential of America. This potential will be actualized through the force of a great literature that uses as a setting the plains and prairies of central North America. The prairies assume a similar figurative and thematic centrality, geographic centrality, and structural centrality in *Leaves of Grass*.

## "LAND OF THE PASTORAL PLAINS, THE GRASS-FIELDS OF THE WORLD!"
### The Prairies and Plains in *Leaves of Grass*

The perennial title of Whitman's lifelong poetic work—*Leaves of Grass*—proclaims the significance of grass as a metaphor. The title is symbolic of life's cyclical regeneration, of the equality of life and death, and of the transcendence of the material into the spiritual. *"What is the grass?"* Whitman asks in section 6 of "Song of Myself" (Whitman's emphasis). Rather, "a child" poses the question. Whitman answers. At first he is evasive: "How could I answer the child? I do not know what it is any more than he." Then, in one line that stands alone, he begins to answer, tentatively and figuratively: "I guess it must be the flag of my disposition, out of hopeful green stuff woven." As Whitman becomes continually more certain of what the grass signifies, this section resounds with metaphorical echoes. Like his poems, Whitman's grass is a text to be interpreted: "it is a uniform hieroglyphic" (*LG* 34). Like America, it is common and democratic. The "handkerchief of the Lord," it is also spiritual (*LG* 33).

The prairies in *Leaves of Grass* also take on these metaphorical echoes to become figuratively and thematically central in some poems and in the volume as a whole. References to the prairies permeate *Leaves of Grass;* the prairies represent the unity of all humankind and of the cosmos because they connect the American East and West and because America is, in turn, the bridge connecting the Old and the New Worlds. A spiritual evolution in *Leaves of Grass* complements the prairies' figurative, thematic, and structural centrality. The prairies ultimately represent humankind's relationship with God and humankind's immortality. They become a metaphor for unlimited human potential—that is, human perfection.

"For You O Democracy" and "Our Old Feuillage" demonstrate how the prairies are structurally central in individual poems. "For You O Democracy" is a short, eleven-line poem that opens with a proclamation of North American unity. Whitman boasts his own role as poet-creator in making this unity:

> Come, I will make the continent indissoluble,
> I will make the most splendid race the sun ever
> shone upon,
> I will make divine magnetic lands. (*LG* 117)

At the end he reiterates that he will accomplish this unity through his poems:

> For you these from me, O Democracy, to serve you
> ma femme!
> For you, for you I am trilling these songs.

Between these statements of enclosure—exactly central at line 6— Whitman punctuates the line end with the image of the prairies: "I will plant companionship thick as trees along all the rivers of America, and along the shores of the great lakes, and all over the prairies." A compact salute to democracy and a direct association of poetry with democracy, the poem also metaphorically associates the prairies, poetry, and democracy. It is a statement that the themes of democracy are the core of the prairie metaphor.

Similarly, "Our Old Feuillage" places the image of the plains and prairies at the center of the poem. Whitman mentions the prairies three times here—once near the beginning (line 9), once near the end (line 78), and once in the middle (line 44). While in the first reference the "prairies" are cited among a list of other landscapes, in the last reference the word "Plains" is capitalized and placed at the end of a line for emphasis. The central reference is inclusive of the surrounding geography of the poem (it unites the images in lines 9 and 78), as the plains are inclusive of the surrounding geography of America: "The scout riding on horseback over the plains west of the Mississippi, he ascends a knoll and sweeps his eyes around" (*LG* 173). The visual act emphasizes that the plains are the center from which all America can be viewed. The central plains are clearly associated with democracy again here, for Whitman writes that this poem is a "compact, the-whole-surrounding, *National Poem*" (*LG* 170–71, note; Whitman's emphasis).

Just as "For You O Democracy" and "Our Old Feuillage" demonstrate the centrality of the prairies in individual poems, so too does "Drum-Taps" demonstrate the prairies' structural, thematic, and figurative centrality in *Leaves of Grass*. That for Whitman the Civil War is central to American history is substantiated by his numerous references to the Civil War in *Leaves of Grass*. While "Origins of Attempted Secession" reveals his obsession with the war, his prefaces to editions of his poetry demonstrate that he sees the war theme as integral to *Leaves of Grass*. The preface to *As a Strong Bird on Pinions Free* (1872) and the preface to the two-volume Centennial Edition of *Leaves of Grass* and *Two Rivulets* (1876) imply the importance of the war to his poetry.[7] "A Backward Glance o'er Travel'd Roads" makes the connection explicit:

> It is certain, I say, that, although I had made a start before, only from the occurrence of the Secession War, and what it show'd me as by flashes of lightning, with the emotional depths it sounded and arous'd . . . —that

only from the strong flare and provocation of that war's
sights and scenes the final reasons-for-being of an au-
tochthonic and passionate song definitely came forth.
. . . Without those three or four years . . . , "Leaves of
Grass" would not now be existing. (*Prose* 2:724)

Whitman's statements in these pieces fortify Gay Wilson
Allen's summary of the war's significance to Whitman: "Whitman
regarded the war to preserve the Union as one of the unavoidable
delays in the 'Years of the Unperformed' before America, and even-
tually the whole world, could fulfill his dream of a new era in which
tyrants would fall and 'crowns grow dim' and there would be 'but
one heart to the globe.'"[8] The war and "Drum-Taps" are figu-
ratively central, therefore, to *Leaves of Grass,* and they are obviously
structurally and thematically central, too, since the "Drum-Taps"
section is inserted at the middle of the Deathbed Edition. Whitman
writes about the relationship of this section to the whole volume:
"the whole book, indeed, revolves around that four years' war,
which, as I was in the midst of it, becomes, in 'Drum-Taps,' pivotal
to the rest entire" (*Prose* 2:469).

Five of the forty-three poems in "Drum-Taps" mention the
prairies specifically in order to stress the importance of the Union.
"Eighteen Sixty-One" emphasizes the Union by implying the gath-
ering of armed men through the figure of the personified year march-
ing across the continent. Before citing smaller geographic areas, the
poem introduces the major sections of the nation—the East, West,
and center, where the year is "with large steps crossing the prairies
out of Illinois and Indiana" (*LG* 282). Two references to the nurtur-
ing fields of grain in the central states appear in "Song of the Banner
at Daybreak" (*LG* 287, 289). In each case the images are among
citations of other geographic areas, stressing the importance of unity
for the nation. While the prairies are again cited as one of many
geographic areas in "Rise O Days from Your Fathomless Deeps," they
are associated with the human heart, the core of one's life, since the
speaker "slept on their breast" (*LG* 291). The soldiers who come to
the defense of the Union in the satirical poem "Virginia—The West"

come only from the "prairies," and significantly they appear in the center of the poem—in the second of the three stanzas (*LG* 293–94). Coming from the center of the Union, the heart of democracy, these prairie soldiers represent loyalty to the Union.

The last poem in "Drum-Taps," "To the Leaven'd Soil They Trod," punctuates the section by celebrating the reunion of North and South. The poem ends with this reconciling image: "The Northern ice and rain that began me nourish me to the end, / But the hot sun of the South is to fully ripen my songs" (*LG* 327). The line immediately preceding these two lines associates the focus throughout the poem on a central and averaging soil specifically with the prairies—a landscape that symbolizes reunion: "The prairie draws me close, as the father to bosom broad the son." This symbolic capacity of the prairies is emphasized in the poem with another specific prairie reference and a generalized reference to the Western soil: the poet sings "to the plains of the poems of heroes, to the prairies spreading wide" (*LG* 327), and he sings "to the leaven'd soil of the general Western world to attest my songs" (*LG* 327). The soil of the vast expanse of the open West, the soil of America, is now "leaven'd"—enlivened and adorned with leaves again. It is now the "average earth," distributed proportionately, equitably. The Union is stronger for that averaging, and the prairie is the symbolic center of this "leaven'd soil."

"Drum-Taps" shows how the prairies are structurally central to Whitman's *Leaves of Grass*, and it indicates the prairies' figurative centrality to both Whitman's text and to America. Whitman uses the words *prairie* or *prairies* forty-five times in his poetry and the word *plains* fourteen times, according to Edwin Harold Eby's *Concordance of Walt Whitman's "Leaves of Grass" and Selected Prose Writings*. While a high concentration of these uses of the words are in "Drum-Taps," references to the prairies are spread throughout *Leaves of Grass*, as the grass is pervasive on the earth's surface. Such pervasiveness indicates the extent to which the prairies are thematically and figuratively central in *Leaves*. The first mentions of prairies in *Leaves of Grass* are important, therefore, not merely because they are the first, but because the poems in which they appear, "Starting from Paumanok" and "Song of Myself," have particular importance to the whole of *Leaves of Grass*.

In the structure of *Leaves* (from the 1860 edition through the Deathbed Edition of 1891–92) "Starting from Paumanok" serves as an introduction, announcing themes and images that recur throughout the book.[9] In his brief introductory work *Walt Whitman*, James E. Miller, Jr., identifies the poem's importance very precisely. He claims that the 1860 edition of *Leaves* takes the form that the book will "eventually . . . assume permanently." "Proto-Leaf" (the title of "Starting from Paumanok" in the 1860 edition) replaces "Song of Myself" (then titled "Walt Whitman") as the first poem. Even the famous 1855 preface is removed, so "Proto-Leaf" stands first in *Leaves of Grass* (1860). Miller explains: "As its original title suggested, this poem was archetypal for the entire book—the pattern leaf on which all the others were modeled: it presented in embryonic form all of the themes and the major images of the book. Whitman's later additions to the poem indicate that he wanted it to serve as a gathering place and point of departure for all the melodies on which he was later to work variations."[10] "Starting from Paumanok" announces the American themes that *Leaves of Grass* associates with the prairies, and the prairies are one of the most important images the poem introduces.

The speaker of "Starting from Paumanok" strikes out on a figurative journey West across the New World. In the first section he introduces the geographical areas and places that he encounters, from Paumanok and Mannahatta to "southern savannas" and California. Roughly midway between Paumanok and California are the vast plains and prairies of central North America, of which the singer is very conscious. He is "aware of the buffalo herds grazing the plains, the hirsute and strong-breasted bull" (*LG* 16).

Whitman begins section 2 with the following list:

> Victory, union, faith, identity, time,
> The indissoluble compacts, riches, mystery,
> Eternal progress, the kosmos, and the modern reports.
> (*LG* 16)

He establishes the themes of the New World, of which the prairies and plains will prove to be an integral part.

In the next section, in fact, Whitman establishes the geographical and figurative centrality of the prairies. The section reads:

> Americanos! conquerors! marches humanitarian!
> Foremost! century marches! Libertad! masses!
> For you a programme of chants.
>
> Chants of the prairies,
> Chants of the long-running Mississippi, and down to
>     the Mexican sea,
> Chants of Ohio, Indiana, Illinois, Iowa, Wisconsin
>     and Minnesota,
> Chants going forth from the centre from Kansas, and
>     thence equidistant,
> Shooting in pulses of fire ceaseless to vivify all.
> (LG 17)

Announcing his program of poems in *Leaves*, Whitman focuses on the geographical center of the United States. All the states mentioned are prairie states. Their geographical position, then, prefigures the symbolic and structural centrality of the plains and prairies in *Leaves of Grass*. Kansas's being the exact center of America, according to the speaker, further highlights the significance of the speech Whitman composed for the Kansas State Silver Wedding celebration. Whitman's chants will pulse out, like blood, from the heart of America to enliven the entire United States with a vital heat.

Section 4 also emphasizes the poetic and geographical center of America. Because his poems figuratively spread from the center, Whitman puns, "Take my leaves America, take them South and North, / . . . Surround them East and West, for they would surround you" (*LG* 17). The geographical center of the United States has vast metaphorical significance for Whitman's poems.

Near the end of the poem, in the catalog of section 14, Whitman mentions the prairies or plains three times. In one instance he is merely "crossing the prairies." In another he emphasizes again the life-supporting nature of the landscape by associating the "plains" with the "spinal river" (*LG* 25), the Mississippi that in *Specimen Days* is uniquely important to American literature. But this landscape and the "Libertad!" that it represents is not limited to the United States, for America is the hope of the world's future. As Whitman puts it, this region is the "land of the pastoral plains, the grass-fields of the world! land of those sweet interminable plateaus!" (*LG* 24)

In the penultimate section of the poem, section 18, Whitman implies the importance of the center of the United States again. This section summarizes the poem (immediately before Whitman addresses very personal words to the reader), so the allusions to the prairies, the telegraph, the Atlantic cable, and the transcontinental railroad become especially important. Telling us what to "see" in his poems, Whitman says, "see, beyond the Kaw, countless herds of buffalo feeding on short curly grass." What the prairies let us see if we look beyond them is the bridging capacity of America. Associating "pulses" in the Atlantic between America and Europe with the telegraph wires spanning the continent, Whitman celebrates the American telegraph system and the transatlantic cable— the joining of the lines of communication around the world. He writes in "Starting from Paumanok": "see, the electric telegraph stretching across the continent, / See, through Atlantica's depths pulses American Europe reaching, pulses of Europe duly return'd." In the next line, the image of the train traversing the prairies further anticipates "Passage to India," as well as "To a Locomotive in Winter": "See, the strong and quick locomotive as it departs, panting, blowing the steam-whistle" (*LG* 27). America becomes a bridge between East and West in "Passage to India," and the last part of the bridge is built, according to "Starting from Paumanok," over the North American plains and prairies. The telegraph lines across the prairies, the mode of oral communication, connect East and West, as the transcontinental railroad offers a way to physically cross this last dividing frontier between people of the Old World and the New.

If "Starting from Paumanok" is an introduction to *Leaves of Grass*, "Song of Myself" is the opening poem of the part that Miller calls the "Gigantic Embryo or Skeleton of Personality." This poem is the "delineation of an archetypal personality for the New World."[11] While the references to prairies and plains in "Song of Myself" are not so assertive as they are in "Starting from Paumanok," they are integral to this "archetypal personality," as shown by their being scattered throughout the poem.

Whitman introduces the concept of vastness early in "Song of Myself." In section 2 he asks the reader, "Have you reckon'd a thousand acres much? have you reckon'd the earth much?" (*LG* 30). He challenges the notion that physical space is a means of measuring one's existence. Vastness is, rather, a cosmic notion—and the prairies come to represent that spiritual vastness or inclusiveness. "Stop this day and night with me and you shall possess the origin of all poems," he writes, "You shall possess the good of the earth and sun, (there are millions of suns left)" (*LG* 30). A thousand acres, the entire earth, is not much. These geographical areas are instead indicative of the cosmic vastness, which contains "millions of suns"—a vastness that the poet will not only show us, but through his poems will guide us to our own communion with: "You shall not look through my eyes either, nor take things from me, / You shall listen to all sides and filter them from your self" (*LG* 30).

One way of understanding, of filtering "your self," is to interpret the meaning of the grass. Whitman first defines the grass in section 6. That definition is, of course, not complete—the definition of a symbol is never complete. But Whitman does not shy from directly handling the symbol, and an examination of section 6 of the poem is necessary to one's understanding of what *grass* signifies and what the prairies signify.

I have said that Whitman is at first tentative in his answer to the child's question, "*What is the grass?*" His boldness grows in this section, however, until he can associate the grass with a transcendent spirituality. After his first answer, in which he guesses, he continues to surmise: "Or I guess it is the handkerchief of the Lord" (*LG* 33). Though Whitman begins two more lines of this section with the tentative statement, "Or I guess . . . ," he becomes bolder and bolder. One notices his growing certainty in echoes like, "hand-kerchief of the Lord" and "Or I guess it is a uniform hieroglyphic" (*LG* 34). His increasing boldness allows Whitman to proclaim a transcendent victory over death at the end of the section: "All goes onward and outward, nothing collapses, / And to die is different from what any one supposed, and luckier" (*LG* 35).

Section 6 reveals still more metaphorical echoes of Whit-man's grass. The grass is "itself a child." It is the "beautiful uncut hair of graves." It is used by the poet. It is associated with the "breasts of young men," with the "mother's lap," with the "beards of old men," with the "faint red roofs of mouths." The grass "means."

Grass is thought-provoking: it leads to the discovery of knowledge. The child questions what the grass is, and immediately the speaker also questions, "How could I answer the child?" The grass is an epistemological force, for the speaker does not "know" what the grass is any more than does the boy, but the speaker starts then to surmise and learn what the grass is.

While knowledge comes to the speaker with his guesses as to the significance of the grass, familiar themes begin to sound. The first line to stand alone—"I guess it must be the flag of my dispo-sition, out of hopeful green stuff woven"—makes at least four im-portant associations. "Flag" suggests the nationalistic tendency of *Leaves*. "My disposition" asserts the self as a major theme. Hope is part of the essence of the grass. Finally, the interweaving suggests the unifying, the democratic, capacity of the symbol, which spreads not only across America and its prairies but over the world as well, linking everything together in its roots and blades. This unifying of *all* introduces the spiritual quality of the symbol, which Whitman makes explicit by saying that "it is the handkerchief of the Lord, / A scented gift and remembrancer designedly dropt." As a "uniform hieroglyphic" it is again a unifying sign of all humanity. The grass signifies the young and old of both sexes, and therefore in another way unifies all humanity. The grass is also the beginning—"itself a child, the produced babe of the vegetation." Thus it signifies ori-gins. It is also, however, representative of endings—death—since it is the "beautiful uncut hair of graves." The grass is finally the great reconciler of life and death—the spiritual unifier of here and hereafter:

> The smallest sprout shows there is really no death,
> And if ever there was it led forward life, and does
>     not wait at the end to arrest it,
> And ceas'd the moment life appear'd.
> All goes onward and outward, nothing collapses,
> And to die is different from what any one supposed,
>     and luckier. (LG 34–35)

In other parts of the poem, too, the grass has spiritual significance. As in *Specimen Days* the grass has a close connection with the metaphysical sky: "This is the grass that grows wherever the land is and the water is, / This the common air that bathes the globe" (LG 45). Further projecting the significance of the grass to the cosmos beyond the "common air that bathes the globe," Whitman writes, "I believe a leaf of grass is no less than the journey-work of the stars" (LG 59). Finally, the spiritual significance of the grass is reiterated in the final section of the poem, when the poet, in a spiritual act, unites himself, the reader, and the grass: "I bequeath myself to the dirt to grow from the grass I love, / If you want me again look for me under your boot-soles" (with a pun on *souls*, LG 89).

Specific references to the prairies in "Song of Myself" function similarly to these general references to grass, underscoring the movement toward the spiritual. References to the physical prairies are incorporated in catalogs, and they do not draw much attention. Writing of the wild animals with which he claims an intimacy, Whitman mentions the "prairie-dog" (LG 40). Wondering about the "friendly and flowing savage," he considers, as one possibility of his own life-style, the "prairie-life" (LG 73). Whereas Whitman's intimacy with the wild animals and men implies a spiritual union, the bridge from the physical to the spiritual is more readily seen in section 33. Whitman transcends time and space at the beginning of the section:

Space and Time! now I see it is true, what I guess'd at,

. . . . . . . . . . . . . . . . . . . . . . . . . . . . . . . . . . .

My ties and ballasts leave me, my elbows rest in sea-
    gaps,
I skirt sierras, my palms cover continents,
I am afoot with my vision. (*LG* 61)

Afoot with his imaginative vision, Whitman catalogs everything he spans in time and space, unifying all things happening in America into one simultaneous instant. Literally near the center of this section, amid the citations of other geographic images is this one: "Where sun-down shadows lengthen over the limitless and lone-some prairie, / Where herds of buffalo make a crawling spread of the square miles far and near" (*LG* 63). While this is a concrete visual image, and in that sense represents a physical aspect of the prairie, the "crawling spread of the square miles" and the "limitless[ness]" of the landscape suggest a metaphorical interpretation—particularly so when the image is part of a transcendental and encompassing vision.

Like "Song of Myself," "When Lilacs Last in the Dooryard Bloom'd" also clearly demonstrates the association between the prairies, America, and Whitman's movement to the spiritual. It is also a particularly apt poem to demonstrate the prairies' structural centrality in the text and their figurative, thematic, and cultural centrality in America. This poem is structurally central because it immediately follows the "Drum-Taps" section at the center of *Leaves of Grass*.

The grass is specifically associated with the prairies in "Li-lacs" since it is back to the prairies that Lincoln's body is being borne. Geographically central, the prairies physically unite the nation, as Lincoln reunited it (lines 74–77 and 89–92, *LG* 332–33). The prairie as metaphor for the unity of America is extended in the death carol, the poem within the poem. Recalling an earlier image of the sea breezes meeting on the prairies, the carol ends with the ocean-prairie analogy in order to imply the eternal presence of the dead president (lines 159–62, *LG* 335). As the carol unites sky, ocean, and prairies—as it unites life and death—so the transcendent quality of the ocean and prairies, emphasized by the poet's floating above this vast eternity, unites the physical and the metaphysical at the end of this carol to death.

In "Lilacs" the prairies are the center of America, the place from where Lincoln came to reinstate the Union. They are also the place that the poet associates with the victory over death. Later in *Leaves of Grass* this center of America will become the center of the world, of the cosmos. In "Passage to India" the movement to the spiritual, which starts from this prairied center of the world, will reach its climax.

"Passage to India" begins with a celebration of the material world, specifically of technological feats, and soon spirals to the spiritual plane, unifying not only the world but the cosmos. Not only are Life and Death bridged in this poem, however. The soul and God are joined as well. In his 1876 preface Whitman writes of "Passage to India":

> I have reserv'd that poem, with its cluster, to finish and explain much that, without them, would not be explain'd, and to take leave, and escape for good, from all that has preceded them. (Then probably "Passage to India," and its cluster, are but freer vent and fuller expression to what, from the first, and so on throughout, more or less lurks in my writings, underneath every page, every line, everywhere.) (*Prose* 2:464–65)

About the spiritual significance of "Passage to India" he writes later in the same preface: "It was originally my intention, after chanting in 'Leaves of Grass' the songs of the body and existence, to then compose a further, equally needed volume, based on those convictions of perpetuity and conservation which, enveloping all precedents, make the unseen soul govern absolutely at last" (*Prose* 2:466). Even though Whitman had to give up the idea of publishing such a volume separate from *Leaves of Grass*, these statements evince his intent in "Passage to India." Thus the poem stands at the spiritual height of *Leaves of Grass*. Because of its place, the role of the prairies in the poem is significant.

The constituting metaphor of the poem is a bridge. On the first plane this land bridge connects the East and West coasts of North America, uniting the states. On the next plane the bridge connects America, Europe, and India. On the third plane it bridges the world with the cosmos. On the fourth plane it connects physical existence and spiritual existence. Beginning with the geographical and moving to the cosmic and spiritual, therefore, the poem bridges or unites *all*. The prairies are the essential vehicle of this metaphor, for it is the completion of the transcontinental railroad across the vast prairies that allows North America to be the final, historical bridge that completes the "rondure" of the globe.

A few earlier poems in *Leaves of Grass* prepare the way for "Passage to India." "Salut au Monde!" announces America's place in the world, but it does not attain the spiritual heights that "Passage" does later. In "Salut" Whitman, the American poet, encircles the earth, but his poetic vision remains linked to his body. "Facing West from California's Shores" is a short lyric that defines the circular path of humanity around the earth, and America becomes the final rejoining arch in this circle. As in "Salut au Monde!," the spiritual realm in "Facing West" remains unexamined so that the historical, worldly story can be emphasized.

"Song of the Redwood-Tree" also depicts America as the link between East and West, but this poem, which comes between "Salut" and "Facing West," develops further than do those other two poems the transcendent quality of America. The last two sections of the poem show that America is the last arch in the world's rondure. It is also the culmination of "thousands of years" of human history "till now deferr'd." It is the promise "to be fulfill'd" of the human race—the New Eden. America transcends time and space to link the "past" and the "future," the "real and ideal" (*LG* 210).

It is mainly through the voice of the redwood tree, however, that the poem rises to a higher spiritual plane than do "Salut" or "Facing West." Aware that its "term has ended," the tree does not lament its death. Indeed, speaking for all its kind, it welcomes the civilization that will be its demise. All the redwoods transcend death by becoming "absorb'd, assimilated" into the advancing "superber race," which will bring into being the millennial prophecy.

Like "Song of the Redwood-Tree," "Passage to India" draws on the popular notion that human history, and therefore human progress, spread from the Middle East and that it would come full circle through America to Asia. But "Passage to India" is a more spiritual poem than "Song of the Redwood-Tree." It does not merely associate the "real and ideal." It more than accounts for the absorbing and assimilating of condemned physical life with the eternal life that will replace it. It celebrates the bridging of the world with the cosmos, the joining of the soul with God. "Passage to India" is the culmination of the three earlier poems in that it proclaims America to be the final arch, or bridge, uniting all geographies on earth, uniting the earth with the cosmos, and uniting man's soul with God. As the setting of the bridge between America's two coasts, the prairies become the focal point of this unifying metaphor.

Section 1 of "Passage to India" introduces the idea of a physical bridge and implies metaphysical associations as well. The world is both spatially and temporally united. It is spatially united by the three achievements celebrated in the poem—the completion of the Suez Canal, the laying of the Atlantic cable, and the joining of the Union Pacific and Central Pacific railroads. It is temporally united when the New World is "by its mighty railroad spann'd" (LG 411): because this New World is "form'd, impell'd" by the past, the transcontinental railroad has, in effect, joined the past with present. Moreover, the world is spiritually united according to "God's purpose":

> Passage to India!
> Lo, soul, seest thou not God's purpose from the first?
> The earth to be spann'd, connected by network,
> The races, neighbors, to marry and be given in
> marriage,
> The oceans to be cross'd, the distant brought near,
> The lands to be welded together. (LG 412)

Because the poem unites the world spatially, temporally, and spiritually, its transcendent philosophy underscores the soul's significance. As the poet shows the soul the significance of a passage to India, he reveals that America is the culmination of God's Edenic vision. In a grand miscegenational wedding ceremony, the races of the world will be joined and an actual brotherhood will pervade the earth. What allows America this importance is that it is the last land mass west before the rondure of the world is complete.

The prairies unite the American continent because they represent the lands that are "welded together"—for the prairies are welded literally by the iron of the railroad. Section 3 celebrates the geography crossed by the railroad. First in this description are the plains and prairies:

> I see over my own continent the Pacific railroad
>     surmounting every barrier,
> I see continual trains of cars winding along the Platte
>     carrying freight and passengers,
> I hear the locomotives rushing and roaring, and the
>     shrill steam-whistle,
> I hear the echoes reverberate through the grandest
>     scenery in the world,
> I cross the Laramie plains, I note the rocks in
>     grotesque shapes, the buttes. (LG 413)

Continuing West, the railroad bridges the thousands of miles, America's vastness, that the prairies and plains so commonly represent:

> Bridging the three or four thousand miles of land
>     travel,
> Tying the Eastern to the Western sea,
> The road between Europe and Asia. (LG 414)

America has thus completed the "rondure of the world."

Whitman quickly extends this definition of *rondure* from a global perspective to a cosmic perspective. Before section 5, the reader and the poet view parts of the earth from a relatively close proximity, but in section 5 Whitman capitalizes *Rondure* and shifts the frame of reference so that the earth is viewed from far off in the cosmos in its circular orbit around the sun:

> O vast Rondure, swimming in space,
> Cover'd all over with visible power and beauty,
> Alternate light and day and the teeming spiritual
>     darkness,
> Unspeakable high processions of sun and moon and
>     countless stars above. (*LG* 414)

The circular patterns in the poem recall Emerson's essay "Circles," and in fact Whitman's "use of Rondure (through which he links man to his source in God) is similar to Emerson's concept of spiritual growth in 'Circles.'"[12] The progression of this spiritual growth has been carefully laid out so far: the prairies have unified America; America has unified the world both spatially and temporally; the poet has unified the world with the cosmos; now the world will unify man's soul with God.

Whitman expounds on this spiritual union for the remainder of the poem. In the last section the poet glorifies the soul's ecstasy in its union with God. The soul is casting off to the metaphorical and spiritual sea:

> O my brave soul!
> O farther farther sail!
> O daring joy, but safe! are they not all the seas of
>     God?
> O farther, farther, farther sail! (*LG* 421)

This section also lists landscapes that now have full metaphorical significance because they are not merely the places from which the poet began early in the poem; they are the incarnations of the spiritual essence that is celebrated at the end of the poem. The poet rejoices:

Passage to more than India!
O secret of the earth and sky!
Of you O waters of the sea! O winding creeks and
    rivers!
Of you O woods and fields! of you strong mountains
    of my land!
Of you O prairies! of you gray rocks!
O morning red! O clouds! O rain and snows!
O day and night, passage to you! (*LG* 420)

The prairies have advanced from being the setting of the transcontinental railroad's completion to being the setting of the union of Old and New, of East and West; to being the focus of the world bridge, the rondure; to being the completing arch of a circle that allows the world to be the Rondure that unites man's soul with God. Finally, they are a spiritual landscape, of which the soul can discover the secret—as it can discover the "secret of the earth and sky."

Soaring to spiritual heights, the group of poems containing "Passage to India" is a climax of *Leaves of Grass*. Following it is a cluster of poems that sustains the spiritual themes. "Whispers of Heavenly Death" explores the "'unknown region' of spiritual law and the acceptance of death as a fulfillment and a new beginning" (*LG* 440 note). Whitman begins the cluster where "Passage to India" left off. The first poem in this group, "Darest Thou Now O Soul," begins:

Darest thou now O soul,
Walk out with me toward the unknown region,
Where neither ground is for the feet nor any path to
    follow?
No map there, nor guide. (*LG* 441)

The prairies become such an unknown region in a later poem in this group—"Night on the Prairies."

Because "Night on the Prairies" first appeared in the 1860

edition of *Leaves of Grass* and was written before Whitman's trip west, it reveals his imaginative, metaphorical conception of the prairies—for the prairies were to Whitman at the time of the poem's composition an imagined, rather than a real, place. The speaker of the poem is camping on the prairies with some western emigrants. After supper, while the others are retiring for the night, he walks off by himself and gazes at the stars. The vast prairies are the earth's reflection of the eternity in the night sky and of the unknown region that the soul contemplates. The speaker's simple, initial action of gazing at the stars culminates in a transcendent understanding of death, one more profound than the Redwood's understanding because the speaker in this poem anticipates a more complete knowledge of his spiritual self after death.

The speaker in "Night on the Prairies" immediately distinguishes himself from the other emigrants as a stargazer. While the others wrap themselves in their blankets to sleep, he walks away from camp. In addition to this action of isolation, he conceives of himself as separate from the "emigrants," to whom he refers as if he is not one of them. This separation from the rest of humanity present on the scene signals the speaker's movement inward. Through this introspection, which will become soul searching, the speaker implies a figurative significance in the stars.[13] He begins to express that significance in the first stanza when he says, "I stand and look at the stars, which I think now I never realized before" (*LG* 452).[14] The play on "realized" here is a nice commingling of the real and the imaginative. The speaker more than intellectually understands the stars; with imaginative power he brings them into being. At the same time the stars become not ideal but real—that is, material.

Alone and gazing at the stars, the speaker quickly conjoins with the metaphysical. Like the child in "There Was a Child Went Forth," he becomes his surroundings and thus defies time: the child becomes an object "for many years or stretching cycles of years" (*LG* 364). But unlike the child, the speaker on the prairies does not absorb an *object*. Rather, he leaves the physical realm to absorb the metaphysical: "Now I absorb immortality and peace, / I admire death and test propositions" (*LG* 452). He still defies time, but more profoundly than the child of the poem placed earlier in *Leaves of Grass*.

Having absorbed immortality, the speaker gains a spiritual knowledge as he says, "I was thinking the day most splendid till I saw what the not-day exhibited, / I was thinking this globe enough till there sprang out so noiseless around me myriads of other globes" (*LG* 452). In his place on the prairie, the speaker is surrounded by a myriad of stars, as if he were the center of the universe. With this shift in frame of reference the prairies become the center of the cosmos, the earthly focus of the starry sky. This night sky, furthermore, is *not* simply night sky. It is, rather, "not-day." Whitman's figurative intent is this: the "not-day" is a metaphor for the "unknown region" of "immortality and peace." The prairies, too, as the focus of this "not-day," take on these metaphorical connotations.

The speaker expounds on his transcendence of time and space in the last stanza of this lyric. Filled with "the great thoughts of space and eternity," he "will measure [him]self by them" (*LG* 452). His is no common measure at all (for such would imply limits), but an expansion beyond measurable limits. The speaker is spread through time and space until he knows that, like the different knowledge gained from the symbols of day and "not-day," there is knowledge to be gained from death as well as from life. While he does not call death *not-life*, in the last two lines of the poem he implies his earlier diction by echoing the word "day" and associating it with "life": "O I see now that life cannot exhibit all to me, as the day cannot, / I see that I am to wait for what will be exhibited by death" (*LG* 453). Death is a spirit journey, something like the poetic journey that the speaker has taken in this poem. It is a total absorption into the cosmos, into "immortality and peace"—an absorption that is reflected in the poem's imaginative movement and in its setting on the prairies.

In the section immediately after "Whispers of Heavenly Death," "From Noon to Starry Night," the poem "To a Locomotive in Winter" reiterates the movement from earth to sky and points out the significant relationship between the prairies and Whitman's transcendental vision and poems. That relationship is emphasized in other poems as well: "When Lilacs Last in the Dooryard Bloom'd," section 2 of "By Blue Ontario's Shores," "As Consequent, etc.," "The Return of the Heroes," and "I Thought That Knowledge Alone Would Suffice." The death carol within "When Lilacs Last in the Dooryard Bloom'd," for example, is a self-reflective comment on poetry in a poem that is linked closely with the prairies, the Union, and a spiritual transcendence of death.

In "To a Locomotive in Winter" the locomotive is being exalted, being summoned, "for once," into the service of "the Muse" (LG 472). In the last eight lines of the poem, as the locomotive's place in poetry becomes the subject, the prairies become associated with Whitman's poetry *and* with the spiritual skies. Outrightly stating the machine's appropriate place in his poetry, Whitman extolls:

> Fierce-throated beauty!
> Roll through my chant with all thy lawless music,
>     thy swinging lamps at night,
> Thy madly-whistled laughter, echoing, rumbling like
>     an earthquake, rousing all,
> Law of thyself complete, thine own track firmly
>     holding,
> (No sweetness debonair of tearful harp or glib piano
>     thine,)
> Thy trills of shrieks by rocks and hills return'd,
> Launch'd o'er the prairies wide, across the lakes,
> To the free skies unpent and glad and strong. (LG 472)

As the speaker would have it, like Whitman's poetry, the locomotive is powerful, beautiful, and unique.

The locomotive is "Launch'd o'er the prairies wide, across the lakes, / To the free skies unpent and glad and strong" (LG 472). The machine is not misplaced in this vast wilderness, but it blends with it, symbolizing in Leo Marx's words Whitman's "wholehearted tribute to this industrialized version of the pastoral ideal."[15] Whitman's association of his poetry with the prairies, then, is clear. His poems, like the locomotive, are "launch'd o'er the prairies"—"America's Characteristic Landscape" and metaphor for an expanding democracy—upward "to the free skies" of a poetic ideal.

The movement from the prairies to the skies, "unpent and glad and strong," is also a movement to the spiritual realm. Thus, like the locomotive, both Whitman's poems and the image of the prairies become associated with the metaphysical. These last eight lines of the poem form a transcendental unity of locomotive, poetry, prairies, and spirit. The prairies in this equation are the common denominator, since they form the physical landscape that allows the locomotive to transcend to the metaphysical skies and the imaginative landscape of America's pastoral ideal, which allows Whitman's poems to transcend to the democratic "free skies unpent and glad and strong." "To a Locomotive in Winter," more successfully and artistically than any other of his poems, equates the prairies, America, the spiritual realm, and Whitman's poetry.

"Songs of Parting" is the resolution and farewell of *Leaves of Grass*. The rest is annexes. In this conclusion "Song at Sunset" is a celebration of an entire life, and Whitman associates some specific places with his life—not the least of which are the Mississippi River (which in *Specimen Days* he connects with the prairies) and the prairies themselves. The stanza making the associations between landscapes and the poet begins by citing these two places. The only other areas mentioned are "cities," "woods," the two seas, and Chicago. Remarkably, Chicago, a prairie city, is mentioned instead of Paumanok or Mannahatta. Whitman is concentrating on the center of America, between the "Eastern Sea" and the "Western Sea," in order to make his song of parting inclusive of all America. The prairies and the Mississippi River, which have a special place in American literature according to *Specimen Days*, become the locus of this farewell poem to America.

The final poem entirely about the prairies to be included in *Leaves of Grass* is also a sunset poem—"A Prairie Sunset." Appearing in the "First Annex: Sands at Seventy," the poem is a more vivid description of a sunset than is "Song at Sunset."[16] It carries with it the jubilation of the earlier sunset poem, but the spiritual connotations of the latter poem are more profound and far-reaching.

The poem reads:

Shot gold, maroon and violet, dazzling silver,
emerald, fawn,
The earth's whole amplitude and Nature's multiform
power consign'd for once to colors;
The light, the general air possess'd by them—colors
till now unknown,
No limit, confine—not the Western sky alone—the
high meridian—North, South, all,
Pure luminous color fighting the silent shadows to
the last. (LG 530–31)

The relationship between the prairie and the metaphysical sky is clearly stated in the title itself. The vastness of the prairies is interpreted as "earth's whole amplitude and Nature's multiform power," which are in turn "consign'd . . . to color," "the general air possessed by them." The movement in the poem is obviously from earth to sky, from the material to the ethereal. The colors were previously unknown, as if through them some glimpse and understanding of the spirit is now revealed. On this spiritual plane there is "no limit, [nor] confine." We are no longer contemplating the "Western sky alone," but the "high meridian—North, South, *all*" (my emphasis). The limitless expansion includes the universal and the spiritual. Finally, the color is "pure," and it is a symbol of eternal good that fights the "silent shadows to the last." Familiar associations appear: vastness, limitlessness, physical conjoining metaphysical, eternity. This final poem of the prairies summarizes the major associations with the prairies in Whitman's poetry. The prairies here exist entirely in the realm of the ideal, now actualized.

Whitman's concept of the prairies remained consistent throughout his poetic career. He originally conceived of them as an ideal region that contained all the potential for good that America itself symbolized. He saw in them the great themes of democracy: freedom, equality, hope, and the realization of a spiritual ideal among them. With his inclination toward the literary arts, he associated the prairies with a national literature that he himself helped to create. His own visit to the prairies in 1879 merely reinforced his preconception: the prairies were, in fact, "America's Characteristic Landscape."

Reaping the harvest of the prairie metaphor, Whitman assumes the same nationalistic themes that are developed by Bryant and the other popular poets. He does not, however, isolate his references to the prairies to a few poems. Rather, they are sown throughout his one, growing poetic work. Whitman's prairies, therefore, spread throughout his poetry as the grass spreads over the earth, unifying all in a great democratic, millennial vision. They symbolize the centrality of America to the world throughout a world history, and they symbolize the centrality of America to the cosmos and the spiritual realm. In Whitman the metaphor grows from the nationalistic vision of the popular poets to a full vision of freedom, equality, and hope for all humankind. The American plains and prairies are "the grass-fields of the world!" The power that is represented in the grass, the power that unites humankind, is a spiritual power: the prairies are indeed the "handkerchief of the Lord," "out of hopeful green stuff woven," which show that "to die is different from what any one supposed, and luckier."

# CHAPTER SIX

# HISTORY AND POETRY

In *A Short History of the United States* (1913) John Spencer Bassett still embraces the dominant nineteenth-century conception of American history:

> In this book I have sought to tell clearly and impartially the story of human achievement in what is now the United States. . . . Those [facts] have been recounted which seem best suited to explain the progress of the people as a nation. . . . From the end of the colonial period the dominant interest is the progress of events which have to do with the common cause of independence, and after that with national development.[1]

Writing what he asserts is "in the most vital sense a social history" because it discusses not only political institutions but also the "social progress of the people," Bassett links that conception of American history with the nation's conception of itself. The historian's attitude also clearly reflects a poetic attitude toward America that is displayed in the prairie and plains metaphor: (1) the "story" of the United States is the story of all "human achievement"; (2) that story is one of affirmative progress; and (3) freedom, "independence," is a unifying factor.

George Bancroft's *History of the Colonization of the United States* also reveals parallels between the prairie metaphor and the popular attitude toward United States history. Bancroft particularly represents the dominant historical attitude because he published his ten-volume *History* over the middle half of the nineteenth century, from 1834 to 1874, and because, according to Russel B. Nye, he "became the American public's favorite historian of its past and the popular prophet of its future."[2]

Like Bassett, Bancroft is concerned with the United States' role in the world. Bancroft begins the introduction to his first volume as follows: "The United States of America constitute an essential portion of a great political system, embracing all the civilized nations of the earth. At a period when the force of moral opinion is rapidly increasing, they have the precedence in the practice and the defense of the equal rights of man." This passage also asserts Bancroft's belief in the primary importance of freedom to American history—a belief that he argues in the preface to his first volume, writing, "The spirit of the colonies demanded freedom from the beginning." Moreover, whereas Bassett generalizes about progress, Bancroft particularizes. His introduction asserts: "While the nations of Europe aspire after change, our constitution engages the fond admiration of the people, by which it has been established. Prosperity follows the execution of even justice; invention is quickened by the freedom of competition; and labor rewarded with sure and unexampled returns."[3]

Like Bassett's and Bancroft's histories, Alexis de Tocqueville's *Democracy in America* (1835, 1840) reflects a concern with the relationship between America and the world, implying that America is representative of a broader human *progress*. He writes in his "Introductory Chapter": "I then turned my thoughts to our own hemisphere, where I imagined that I discerned something analogous to the spectacle which the New World presented to me. I observed that the equality of conditions is daily progressing towards those extreme limits which it seems to have reached in the United States, and that the democracy which governs the American communities appears to be rapidly rising into power in Europe."[4]

Tocqueville furthermore demonstrates other ideological points that are incorporated into the poetic metaphor. The thesis of his work focuses on equality. "The more I advanced in the study of American society," he writes, "the more I perceived that the equality of conditions is the fundamental fact from which all others seem to be derived, and the central point at which all my observations constantly terminated" (1:3). He also maintains that a democracy "impart[s] . . . a novel character" to the "idea of [human] perfectibility": "In proportion as castes disappear and the classes of society approximate—as manners, customs, and laws vary, . . . —as new facts arise—as new truths are brought to light—as ancient opinions are dissipated, and others take their place—the image of an ideal perfection, forever on the wing, presents itself to the human mind" (2:34, 35).

The prevalent cultural notion of progress that these historians demonstrate implies manifest destiny. Four nineteenth-century historians, Bancroft among them, reflect the pervasiveness of this political and economic tool. In his *Condensed Geography and History of the Western States or the Mississippi Valley* (1828) Timothy Flint writes:

> It is no crime of the present civilized races, that inhabit these regions, that their forefathers came over the sea, and enclosed lands, and cut down trees, where the Indians had hunted and fought. If they will not, and can not labor, and cultivate the land, and lead a municipal life, they are in the same predicament with a much greater number of drunkards, idlers and disturbers of society, who are a charge and a burden upon it in all civilized communities. Like them, they ought to be treated with tenderness; to be enlightened and reclaimed, if possible; and, as far as may be, to be restrained from hurting us, and each other. But it is surely as unjust, as it is preposterous, to speak of the prevalence of our race over theirs, as an evil; and from a misjudging tenderness to them, do injustice to our own country, and *the cause of human nature*.[5]

Like Flint, Henry Howe provides a revealing view of the ethnocentricity that allowed Europeans to claim the lands of the Native Americans, and also like Flint, Howe relates that appropriation of the natives' lands to a human progress. In the preface to his *Historical Collections of the Great West* (1854) Howe concludes a brief, laudatory, and melodramatic sketch of white settlement in America with this:

> The settlements of the pale faces rapidly advance. They reach the ocean-ward slope of the mountains. They pass over their summits. The smokes of their cabins curl up in the western valleys. The red man vanishes before them. Civilization is his conqueror, and now the footsteps of millions of the new race press his grave and press the graves of his fathers.
>
> To contemplate these mighty events—more wondrous than Romance—is instructive to Virtue!—to act well in the Present, its aim!—to anticipate more glorious changes in the Future, its brightest Hope!"[6]

Bancroft sounds a similar note at the end of the introduction of his first volume. He characterizes the continent before European settlement as an "unproductive waste," whose only "inhabitants were a few scattered tribes of feeble barbarians, destitute of commerce and of political connections" (3–4). Then, to establish the credibility of this historical progress, he asserts the role of God in it: "It is the object of the present work to explain how the change in the condition of our land has been accomplished; and, as the fortunes of a nation are not under the control of blind destiny, to follow the steps by which a favouring Providence, calling our institutions into being, has conducted the country to its present happiness and glory" (4).

Tocqueville, too, is influenced by the idea of a divine providence. "The gradual development of the equality of conditions," he writes, "is . . . a providential fact, and it possesses all the characteristics of a divine decree" (1:6). Whereas Flint, Howe, and Bancroft do not lament the passing of the wilderness or of another race, Tocqueville's attitude is slightly different, however. He definitely believes that Europeans are superior to American Indians: "Amongst these widely differing families of men, the first which attracts attention, the superior in intelligence, in power and in enjoyment, is the white or European, the man pre-eminent" (1:338). But he writes about the destruction of the Indians with a moroseness that implies compassion.

About their "oppression" he writes: "Before the arrival of white men in the New World, the inhabitants of North America lived quietly in their woods, enduring the vicissitudes and practising the virtues and vices common to savage nations. The Europeans, having dispersed the Indian tribes and driven them into the deserts, condemned them to a wandering life full of inexpressible sufferings. . . . European tyranny rendered them more disorderly and less civilized than they were before" (1:339–40). Later, he states that "not only have these wild tribes receded, but they are destroyed" (1:343). Summarizing that destruction, he cites the Europeans' introduction of "fire-arms, ardent spirits, and iron" as the means by which the Indians acquired "new tastes" that deteriorated their old life-style and led to their trading the only things they could that were of value to the whites—furs. "Hence," Tocqueville writes, "the chase became necessary," and "whilst the wants of the natives were thus increasing, their resources continued to diminish" (1:343). This dynamic caused emigrations of the tribes as they were forced to follow their resources, and citing his own witnessing of such movements (which were also, of course, enforced by the United States government), he states, "It is impossible to conceive the extent of the sufferings which attend these forced emigrations" (1:345).

Predicting that "the Indian nations of North America are doomed to perish" (1:347), Tocqueville summarizes the situation:

> With their resources and acquired knowledge, the Europeans soon appropriated to themselves most of the advantages which the natives might have derived from the possession of the soil; they have settled in the country, they have purchased land at a very low rate or have occupied it by force, and the Indians have been ruined by a competition which they had not the means of

resisting. They were isolated in their own country, and their race only constituted a colony of troublesome aliens in the midst of a numerous and domineering people. (1:354–55)

Despite Tocqueville's insights, lamenting the passing of the native Americans and the wilderness is, on the whole, the province of the poetic metaphor of the prairies, not that of contemporary histories. Flint makes this distinction clear when he writes in his *Condensed Geography and History:* "To those, who have predicted, that [the author] would draw too largely upon the language and the coloring of poetry and the imagination, he can only say, that it has been his first aim, to compress the greatest possible amount of *useful information* into the smallest compass" (11; my emphasis). As Bernard Rosenthal further points out, Flint keeps the celebratory vision of the West out of his *History*, denying that it is a place of "spiritual replenishment."[7] Distinguishing between "poetry" (and the imagination) and "useful information," Flint presents what is to him a more realistic attitude, what he assumes (no doubt correctly) is the dominant popular view of American history and progress.

Francis Parkman catches the same difference between the historian's view and the popular poet's dominant conception of the prairies and plains most specifically and completely in *The Oregon Trail* (1849) when he writes:

> Should any one of my readers ever be impelled to visit the prairies, . . . I can assure him that he need not think to enter at once upon the paradise of his imagination. A dreary preliminary, a protracted crossing of the threshold, awaits him before he finds himself fairly upon the verge of the "great American desert"—those barren wastes, the haunts of the buffalo and the Indian, where the very shadow of civilization lies a hundred leagues behind him.
>
> The intervening country, the wide and fertile belt that extends for several hundred miles beyond the ex-

treme frontier, will probably answer tolerably well to his preconceived ideas of the prairie; for that it is from which picturesque tourists, painters, poets, and novelists, who have seldom penetrated farther, have derived their conceptions of the whole region. If he has a painter's eye, he may find his period of probation not wholly void of interest. The scenery, though tame, is graceful and pleasing. Here are level plains, too wide for the eye to measure; green undulations, like motionless swells of the ocean; abundance of streams, followed through all their windings by lines of woods and scattered groves.

But let him be as enthusiastic as he may, he will find enough to damp his ardor. His wagons will stick in the mud; his horses will break loose; harness will give way; and axletrees prove unsound. His bed will be a soft one, consisting often of black mud of the richest consistency. As for food, he must content himself with biscuit and salt provisions; for, strange as it may seem, this tract of country produces very little game. As he advances, indeed, he will see, moldering in the grass by his path, the vast antlers of the elk, and farther on the whitened skulls of the buffalo, once swarming over this now deserted region. Perhaps, like us, he may journey for a fortnight, and see not so much as the hoofprint of a deer; in the spring, not even a prairie hen is to be had.

Yet, to compensate him for this unlooked-for deficiency of game, he will find himself beset with "varmints" innumerable. . . . Add to this, that all the morning, the sun beats upon him with a sultry, penetrating heat, and that, with provoking regularity, at about four o'clock in the afternoon, a thunderstorm rises and drenches him to the skin.[8]

Using most of the images common to the poetic metaphor, Parkman counters a romantic with a realistic view. Later he summarizes the tension between the two views:

With the stream of emigration to Oregon and California, the buffalo will dwindle away, and the large wandering communities who depend on them for support must be broken and scattered. The Indians will soon be abased by whisky and overawed by military posts; so that within a few years the traveler may pass in tolerable security through their country. Its danger and its charm will have disappeared together. (193–94)

Even though this distinction between a romantic view and a realistic view exists between nineteenth-century historians and nineteenth-century popular poets as well, the similarities are nonetheless telling. The bias is nationalist and progressivist—a minor voice recognizes that something is lost. In the histories, that minor voice is even quieter. Yet the image of the prairies and plains in nineteenth-century American poetry clearly corresponds to the dominant cultural ideology. The histories, I would venture to say, display a more progressivist, less "imaginative," attitude than the poetry. They reveal a realistic ideology, that is, one *lived* by the populace. That ideology, then, influenced—controlled—the poetic metaphor.

The prairie metaphor in nineteenth-century American poetry therefore helps to explain various phenomena associated with American culture and literature. It affirms the importance of geographical place and regional culture. It clarifies the relationship between nineteenth-century American ideology and literature—including the roles of democracy, progressivism, slavery, and the treatment of the native population. It reflects the relationships that exist among poetry's audience, theme, and form in a burgeoning democracy—implying, on one hand, that although conventional forms are more viable to a popular audience and for dominant ideological themes, such forms can also embody unpopular statements about the dominant ideology, in which case (Melville's) conventional forms alone will not popularize the poetry; and further implying, on the other hand, that unconventional forms (Whitman's) can be a suitably popular mode of expression when they combine less conventional themes with themes more acceptable to the dominant ideology. The metaphor also demonstrates the irony that the publicly successful poets in a burgeoning democracy and developing country are the ones closest to an older, conventional tradition. It comments, in short, on the relationship between the poet and his or her nation during a formative period for American poetry.

Writing the first significant poem about the prairies, William Cullen Bryant writes one of the first truly American poems. His optimism allows him to associate the prairies and Eden, thus imbuing the prairies with a spiritual significance that during his time became an American literary convention. Beneath this optimism, however, is a melancholic tone. As Bryant acknowledges in "The Prairies," America's fervor for expansion causes it to overrun the native life on the continent, and Bryant is sensitive enough to recognize the loss. His understanding of America's destructive potential gives rise to the ambiguity in the poem, and it enriches the prairie metaphor in the poem. While he is insightful enough to see the tendency in America for destruction, his ideological vision of "imperialist expansion" nevertheless dominates the poem.[9]

Bryant further enriches the prairie metaphor by using it to create poetry that is American. He draws on native American Indian life in "The Prairies" and on Indian myth in "The Painted Cup." By appealing to these native elements, he spurns Old World myths and makes his prairie poems new and unique, like the country that spawned them. Using names specifically associated with the place, he opens the ground for an American poetic language.

Bryant's letters about his trip to Illinois in 1832 reveal his process of idealizing the prairies and demonstrate how he shapes the prairie metaphor according to common attitudes. The letters thus identify that his is indeed a popular voice, and they suggest a similar dynamic of poetic creation for the other popular poets. As those poets reflect common prairie images and echo popular themes, they further cultivate the metaphor. With the exception of Longfellow, however, the other nationally recognized poets do not use the metaphor so fully nor so well as Bryant. They demonstrate nevertheless how popular a subject the prairies are with nineteenth-century Americans. H. and John Hay, writing from the Illinois prairies, nurture the metaphor with regional themes, characters, and dialects. Treating the prairies with some degree of sophistication, they acknowledge the ambiguity but still express a predominantly positive attitude. Alice and Phoebe Cary and Lydia Huntley Sigourney introduce both native and emigrant women into the metaphor and acknowledge the harshness of life on the prairie frontier. John Greenleaf Whittier politicizes the metaphor. The tone of his Kansas poems is not the result of mere nationalism nor patriotism, but of an effort to work a change in society and government. Longfellow's "Evangeline" and "Hiawatha" demonstrate his growing understanding of the depth and richness of the prairie metaphor. Between the writing of those two works, he becomes aware that the prairies are something more than a popular subject: they are a trope that can help cultivate an American literature.

Emily Dickinson glibly, almost flippantly, asserts that a metaphor need not be dominated nor constrained by cultural attitudes. Speaking in a private voice,[10] she focuses on the power of the individual poet's creative imagination. The poet makes her or his own metaphor. Though Herman Melville most likely did not know of Dickinson, he thinks similarly. He extends her implication by creating a prairie metaphor that is exactly the opposite of the predominant, optimistic metaphor. Melville's pessimism sprouts weedlike in this otherwise well cultivated American garden. In the private voice of the poet who has been slighted by democracy, he scorns America for its failed hopes and ideals, disclosing America's failed spiritual quest.

Though the opposition of pessimism and optimism surfaces in Bryant and to lesser degrees in the other popular poets, by and large the public voice is optimistic, the private voice, pessimistic. This split between the public and the private in the American poetic voice reveals the underlying tension created by the democracy. The popular poets side with the popular voice of democracy and perpetuate the millennial concept of America. The poets of the artistic *self*, however, speak of a common democracy that is destructive to the individual. Walt Whitman unites the two attitudes,[11] proclaiming through his prairie metaphor that America is the culmination of the democratic ideal and that the poet's role is to praise that ideal in a popular voice. Because part of that ideal is the full realization of the individual, however, Whitman voices his artistic individuality in a revolutionary form. Structurally and thematically central to *Leaves of Grass*, his prairie metaphor thus represents the centrality of America in a cosmic vision of spiritual unity for all individuals.

Before the discovery of the prairies' literary value, the geography of the American poet was the Eastern Seaboard, mountains, meadows, and some open farmland, but not vast expanses of open grassland. As Bryant points out, there was not even an English word for prairie. As the prairies opened to cultivation and settlement after their discovery and exploration, American poets had to confront that expanse. During a historical period marked by a fervor for the growth of the nation, poets responding to that nationalism associated the conventional American ideals of freedom, equality, hope, and spiritualism with the prairies' openness. This new and unique place, the prairied West, in turn gave new meaning to those conventional notions. This place was different from any other place at any other time in history, so things and ideas associated with it were not only different from, but better than, those comparable things and ideas of the Old World. American freedom was true freedom; American equality, true equality; American spirituality, the ultimate human achievement. Such a millennial vision is not easily comprehended nor explained. Its most appropriate mode is metaphor. The garden metaphor, which had been at hand for American poets since the Puritans emigrated, was revitalized by the prairie metaphor, which nurtured it with the encompassing and open theme of democracy.

When considered comprehensively, the prairie metaphor in nineteenth-century American poetry also reveals the paradoxical characteristics of a burgeoning democracy. The conventional ideals of freedom, hope, equality, future prosperity, spirituality, and a leading place in world history are juxtaposed with destructive tendencies. As white civilization encroaches on the native population and the natural order of the wilderness, the new political and social order overruns the natural order. The romantic values of the wilderness are threatened by racism, overpopulation, and cultivation. In short, the idea of a democracy threatens man's idea of self-worth, as self-worth is defined by man's place in and relationship to nature. Democracy threatens man's idea, that is, of his natural, essential self.

In the prairie metaphor, therefore, nineteenth-century American poets are able to confront the openness of America itself: they can celebrate its potential for good, as well as acknowledge its potential to destroy. Likewise, they can proclaim the equality of the populace, as well as decry the isolation of the individual. The opposition between democracy and the individual furthermore affects the voice of the metaphor as much as it affects the themes. The overwhelming popular enthusiasm for manifest destiny asserts itself in the popular poetic voice of nineteenth-century America. The ideals of the incipient democracy—freedom, equality, hope, spiritualism—reverberate in the prairie poems of Bryant, Holmes, Lowell, the Carys, Sigourney, Whittier, and Longfellow. Dickinson and Melville, however, in their private voices, question this oversimplification of the prairie metaphor. Dickinson's light-humored poem about the making of a prairie implicitly mocks the seriousness of the great themes of the nationalistic metaphor. Melville outrightly challenges the optimistic version of the metaphor and ironically offers its inverse. To him the prairies represent the moral and spiritual degeneration of America. Whitman then reconciles these opposing voices by combining the popular with the individual artistic voice while he uses the prairie metaphor to proclaim and celebrate the self and the unity of America.

As the poets assume these various voices, they make poetic statements about the poet's role in the incipient democracy. The popular poets view themselves as participants in, observers of, and spokesmen for a historical and cultural process. The private poets see themselves as persons cast aside by the cultural mass, and they assume the roles of individual artist, critic, or prophet. The reconciling voice of Whitman, then, becomes all of the above—participant, observer, spokesman, priest, and prophet.

While they define their roles in a democracy, these poets shape an American poetry. Bryant, Longfellow, and the other popular poets unite the essential characteristics of the landscape with common, and predominantly optimistic, American attitudes in formally conventional poems. Dickinson, on the other hand, in formally unconventional poems suggests that the individual poet's imagination creates something entirely new, not that the poet reveals some common, existent attitude. While Melville mainly writes formally conventional poems, his voice remains private in comparison to the overwhelming popular voices, and he makes a separate, and new, metaphor. Whitman reconciles these two extremes: in the unique form of his poetry and in his thematic development of the self in union with the mass, he creates something new, and at the same time in his nationalistically optimistic themes he promulgates common, American attitudes.

The poets included in this study, therefore, are collectively creating a new American poetry. This genesis is characterized by opposition—public versus private, the individual versus the democracy, artistic freedom versus artistic constraints, personal freedom and equality versus slavery, manifest destiny versus genocide, abundance versus destruction, nature versus civilization, nationalism versus internationalism, hope for the future versus spiritual degeneration. Central to these poetic creations are the vast and open prairies, an appropriate landscape for the openness that characterizes this formative period for American poetry and poets.

# NOTES

PREFACE

**1.** I present here a definition, derived from the botanist J. E. Weaver, of the areas with which I am concerned.

Formed about twenty-five million years ago by the uplift of the Rocky Mountains, the vast region stretching along the Rocky Mountains from Texas to Saskatchewan and reaching eastward to northern Indiana was in the nineteenth century characterized mainly by its grasses. This grassland could be divided roughly into two areas: the alluvial lowlands of the Mississippi River Basin and the highlands of the Western Great Plains. Whether called "prairies" or "plains," these grasslands held in common large spaces devoid of trees and covered with grasses. They were (and still are) commonly classified as tall-grass, medium-grass, short-grass, and mixed prairies. In the nineteenth century tall-grass prairies existed in the following areas (the states' names refer to modern boundaries): the northern half of Illinois; all of Iowa; the southwestern and western halves of Minnesota; the northwestern half of Missouri; mid-Oklahoma; the eastern third of Kansas; and the eastern fourth of North Dakota, South Dakota, and Nebraska. Medium-grass prairie covered mid-North Dakota, South Dakota, Nebraska, Kansas, and western Oklahoma. Short-grass prairie covered the eastern third of Montana, the western two-thirds of North Dakota and South Dakota, the western fourth of Nebraska and Kansas, the Oklahoma and Texas panhandles, and the eastern thirds of Colorado and Wyoming.

**2.** I am not assuming that symbol and metaphor are synonyms, but that the reader's processing of the relationship between tenor and vehicle of a metaphor is similar to the processing of the relationship between the symbol as signifier and what is signified. Paul Ricoeur, Mark Turner, and Samuel R. Levin stress that metaphor works primarily on a cognitive level, rather than the semantic or rhetorical levels. In *The Rule of Metaphor,* for example, Ricoeur writes: "Metaphor is the rhetorical process by which discourse unleashes the power that certain fictions have to redescribe reality" (7). See also Turner's *Death Is the Mother of Beauty*, 3–4, and Levin's *Metaphoric Worlds*, 1–2. I also prefer "metaphor" as an encompassing term because we can, I think, say that for most nineteenth-century poets the prairies and plains *are* America.

3. Bachelard, *The Poetics of Space*, xix–xx, 184.

CHAPTER ONE. Exploring the Prairies

1. For convenience of phrasing I will at times use America or American to refer to the United States.

I intend Richard Slotkin's definition of *ideology:* "an abstraction of the system of beliefs, values, and institutional relationships that characterize a particular culture or society" ("Myth and the Productions of History," 70).

2. See chapter 1 of *Westward Expansion*, "The Frontier Hypothesis," for an overview of Ray Allen Billington and Martin Ridge's position. Much of the following historical information is gleaned from Billington's and Ridge's book. Richard White's *It's Your Misfortune and None of My Own: A History of the American West* is also essential to a study of the American West. Particularly relevant here are the sections on land acquisitions (61–84), Indian removal (85–118), and American land policy (137–54).

3. Billington and Ridge, *Westward Expansion*, 413–18, 591–610.

4. White, *It's Your Misfortune*, 74.

5. Ibid., 73.

6. "Human progress" is defined here in both narrow and broad terms: as an individual gaining possession of his own, private land and as an advancement of civilization in the wilderness.

7. Significantly, when introducing this landscape to the reading public in their *History*, Lewis and Clark do not distinguish between prairie and plain. Rather, they use these two words, and their plurals, interchangeably. Describing the "plains" on one side of the river, they state that on the other side "is a similar *prairie* country" (1:50, my emphasis throughout this paragraph). Later they note: "The present season is that in which the Indians go out on the *prairies* to hunt the buffalo; but as we discovered some hunters' tracks, and observed the *plains* on fire in the direction of their villages, we hoped that they might have returned to gather the green Indian corn" (1:54). Still later they write: "Back of this *plain* is a woody ridge about 70 feet above it, at the end of which we formed our camp. This ridge separates the lower from a higher *prairie*" (1:63). Much later they note: "In the evening the *prairie* took fire, either by accident or design, and burned with great fury, the whole *plain* being enveloped in flames" (1:185). As these explorers introduce the prairies to

nineteenth-century Americans, then, they define prairie(s) and plain(s) synonymously—either of the two words (or their plurals) invoking in the reader's mind a vast and open, grassy frontier.

8. McDermott, "Introductory Essay," in Irving, A *Tour on the Prairies*, xv.

9. Antelyes, *Tales of Adventurous Enterprise*, x.

10. Kime, "The Author as Professional," 241.

11. It is interesting to read the following entire paragraph from the "Author's Introduction" to A *Tour on the Prairies* in order to see how Irving uses his literary talents to persuade his readers:

> I make no boast of my patriotism; I can only say, that, as far as it goes, it is no blind attachment. I have sojourned in various countries; have been treated in them above my deserts; and the remembrance of them is grateful and pleasant to me. I have seen what is brightest and best in foreign lands, and have found, in every nation, enough to love and honour; yet, with all these recollections living in my imagination and kindling in my heart, I look round with delightful exultation upon my native land, and feel that, after all my ramblings about the world, I can be happiest at home. (8)

The writer of this paragraph is obviously in control of his audience, as is evident from his deferential acknowledgment of the pleasures of his foreign travels and from his delicate turn to a "delightful exultation" in his "native land." Here is a humble speaker who is "happiest at home." Such a well-crafted voice, sincere or contrived, would persuade the reader whose interests are in the expanses of the burgeoning democracy.

Irving's nationalistic tone is also evident within the body of the book itself. See note 13 below on Irving's politicizing of the prairies.

For further analyses of the relation of A *Tour on the Prairies* to Irving's writing career see Bowden, *Washington Irving*, 145, 149–51, 184, and Cracroft, *Washington Irving: The Western Works*, 10–22.

12. In *Errand into the Wilderness* Perry Miller characterizes the Puritans' conception of their religious purpose in the New World by discussing the biblical links to their actions.

13. In the body of the book itself Irving reasserts the connection between the prairies and the democratic man when he advocates the American counterpart of the European Grand Tour: "We send our youth abroad to grow luxurious and effeminate in Europe; it appears to me, that a previous tour on the prairies would be more likely to produce that manliness, simplicity, and self-dependence, most in unison with our political

institutions" (55). This statement has affinities with Whitman's conception of the prairies as well.

**14.** Irving has difficulty reconciling himself to this practice, however, and he often refers to the wastefulness of discarding good meat.

**15.** Turner, "The Significance of the Frontier," 3, 8.

**16.** Quoted in Lawson-Peebles, *Landscapes and Written Expression*, 9; Watson's emphasis.

**17.** Tuan, *Topophilia*, 5.

**18.** Ibid.

**19.** Slotkin, "Myth and Production of History," 77.

CHAPTER TWO. **Breaking the Sod**

**1.** See Booker, "The Garden Myth," 16, and Wallace, "Prelude to Disaster."

**2.** *Letters* 1:339. Subsequent references in the text are from this edition.

Bryant paid little attention to the mechanics of writing in his letters, especially punctuation. Numerous notations of "sic" in the quotations would be cumbersome.

**3.** The last line of Bryant's essay "Illinois Fifty Years Ago" reads: "What I have thought and felt amid these boundless wastes and awful solitudes [of the prairies] I shall reserve for the only form of expression in which it can be properly uttered" (*Prose* 2:22). Parke Godwin, however, Bryant's son-in-law who edited this essay, was a bad editor of Bryant's letters. He inserted a passage from an 1841 letter into an 1832 letter, and he apparently made up a story about Bryant meeting the young Abraham Lincoln during his visit to Illinois (see *Letters* 1:345, note 5, and 350, note 6). Also, no evidence has been found in Bryant's extant letters to indicate that he wrote the sentence quoted above from "Illinois Fifty Years Ago." Godwin apparently invented that statement, too, or he heard it or something like it spoken by his father-in-law. Godwin, who worked with Bryant at the *Evening Post*, knew his father-in-law well enough to understand his sentiments. That "understanding" does not, of course, mitigate bad editing. But whether or not Bryant actually wrote or spoke this sentence, he does, as his letters show, reserve description of the prairies themselves for the poem.

**4.** Baxter, "William Cullen Bryant," 9.

**5.** Bryant is imposing his knowledge of a contemporary archaeological theory on the memory of his recent experience on the prairies. He wrote about the theory of previous cultivation on the prairies in *A Popular History of the United States*, a four-volume work that he coauthored (see 1:19–34, "The Mound Builders").

6. See also Eby, "Bryant's 'The Prairies.'"

7. *Poems* (New York: D. Appleton, 1876), 184. Unless otherwise noted, all subsequent references in the text are from this edition.

8. Those critics noting Wordsworth's influence on Bryant are Brown, *William Cullen Bryant*, 144–46; Fussell, *Lucifer in Harness*, 113; and McLean, *William Cullen Bryant*, 112–14.

9. A number of articles attest to Bryant's nationalism and civic-mindedness in his poetry: Baxter, "The Dilemma of Progress"; Ferguson, "Creative Context"; Free, "Bryant on Nationalism"; McDowell, "Introduction"; McLean, *William Cullen Bryant*, 85–107, and "Progress and Dissolution in Bryant's Poetry"; and Ralph N. Miller, "Nationalism in Bryant's 'The Prairies.'"

10. See especially pages 1–13, 16–17, 48–55, 123–24, 215–17. See also W. C. Bryant II, "Poetry and Painting."

11. McLean, *William Cullen Bryant*, 113.

12. Erkkila, *Whitman*, 83.

13. See Silber, "Bryant's 'Lectures on Mythology,'" 135–36.

14. Cassirer, *Mythical Thought*, 15; see also Kirk, *Myth*, 10.

15. Silber, "Bryant's 'Lectures on Mythology,'" ii.

16. Kirk concurs that these are two of the most common themes in classical mythology (*Myth*, 10, 189–92). Bryant derived these central themes primarily from his own reading of Ovid, Homer, Virgil, and Apollodorous (see Silber, "Bryant's 'Lectures on Mythology,'" 89).

17. Matthiessen writes about the nineteenth-century American "Need for Mythology" (*American Renaissance*, 626–31). McLean also comments on this need and on the Native American mythological tendencies in "The Painted Cup" (*William Cullen Bryant*, 129).

18. See McLean, *William Cullen Bryant*, 43, on "The Prairies" and the American ideal of "plentitude," and Newlin, *"The Prairie,"* on "The Prairies" and manifest destiny.

19. Of course *prairie* is French, but the word becomes American because of the uniqueness of the place, and the word is obviously not English. Another common non-English word that Bryant uses for *prairie* is *savanna*, which does have a New World origin. He does not use the Anglo-Saxon word *meadow*.

20. Bryant has changed the conventional metaphor of poetic inspiration, which he used in the earlier poem "The West Wind" (1821).

21. Prairie grass in Illinois at the time of Bryant's visit would have been big bluestem, switch grass, and slough grass, all of which averaged a height of five to eight feet and were particular to North America.

22. See Booher, "Garden Myth."

**23.** Bryant had a historian's interest in the Mound Builders. See Dahl, "Mound-Builders," and note 5 above.

**24.** See Brown, *William Cullen Bryant*, 34–38 and Parke Godwin, *A Biography of William Cullen Bryant* 1:24–25, 32–33.

**25.** The opening lines of "The Prairies" in the *Knickerbocker* 2 (December 1833) read:

> These are the Gardens of the Desert, these
> For which the speech of England has no name—
> The boundless unshorn fields, where lingers yet
> The beauty of the earth ere man had sinned—
> The Prairies. (410)

In *Poems* (Boston: Russell, Odiorne, and Metcalf, 1834) 39, they read:

> These are the Gardens of the Desert, these
> The unshorn fields, boundless and beautiful,
> And fresh as the young earth, ere man had sinned—
> The Prairies.

In *Poems* (New York: Harper and Brothers, 1836), they read as I quote them at the beginning of the section on Bryant's prairie poems (with the exception of an uppercase G on "Gardens").

**26.** See also Eby, "Bryant's 'The Prairies'" 356–57.

**27.** Whitman, *Prose Works*, 1:267.

**28.** Donoghue, *Connoisseurs of Chaos*, 11.

### CHAPTER THREE. Tilling, Sowing, and Cultivating

**1.** Griswold, *The Poets and Poetry of America*, 51.

**2.** By "idea of the West," I mean not only the American West beyond the Allegheny Mountains and the Ohio River but also the West as America, which the prairied West also signifies. See Fussell, *Frontier*, 3–25.

**3.** Charvat, *Profession of Authorship*, 46.

**4.** See Coggeshall, *Poets and Poetry of the West*, 77–78, 84–85, on Smith and Finley.

**5.** Stibitz, *Illinois Poets*, 3.

**6.** Ibid., 9.

**7.** Ibid., 12.

**8.** For examples of Matt Field's prairie poems, see Field, *Sante Fe Trail*, 5–46, 93–96, 122–23, 286–88.

In addition to the ones cited in my text, the following newspaper and magazine poets of the West mention the prairies or write entire poems about the prairies: William D. Gallagher of Cincinnati, Isaac H. Julian of Indiana, Alvin Robinson of Illinois, and John J. Piatt of Indiana (see Coggeshall, *Poets and Poetry of the West*, 150–52, 454–55, 588, 667); George P. Morris, Charles Fenno Hoffman, and J. K. Mitchell (see Griswold, *Poets and Poetry of America*, 267, 306–7, 514); R. G. Scott of Iowa, John Banvard (the painter whose pictures of the Mississippi River were the inspiration for Longfellow's attention to that setting in "Evangeline"), Adelaide G. Bennet of Minnesota, Arthur Sheldon Peacock of Indiana and Kansas, and Josiah Moody Fletcher (see Herringshaw, *Local and National Poets*, 188, 280, 519–20, 541, 821–22); and William Ashbury Kenyon, M. H. Jenks, B. F. Stribling, and John Hay, all of Illinois (see Stibitz, *Illinois Poets*, 1–33).

John Howard Bryant of Illinois, John Hay of Illinois, and Thomas Brower Peacock of Kansas published editions of their work and wrote a substantial number of poems associated with the prairied West.

John T. Flanagan's "Poetic Voices in the Early Middle West" is a useful summary about poetry in the early Midwest. Ralph Rusk's *Literature of the Middle Western Frontier* is also worth consulting (1:303–51 and 2:354–62), as is Dorothy Dondore's *The Prairie and the Making of Middle America* (239–87). Bernard F. Engel and Patricia W. Julius have edited *A New Voice for a New People*, a helpful anthology of nineteenth-century midwestern poetry.

**9.** Coggeshall, *Poets and Poetry of the West*, 588.

**10.** Ibid., 667.

**11.** Ibid., 454–55.

**12.** Griswold, *Poets and Poetry of America*, 514.

**13.** John Howard Bryant, *Poems, Written from Youth to Old Age, 1824–1884* (Princeton, Ill.: T. P. Streeter, 1885), 88–89. Subsequent references in the text are from this edition. See also Hallwas, "The Poetry of John Howard Bryant."

**14.** Stiblitz, *Illinois Poets*, 21.

**15.** Ibid., 20.

**16.** John E. Hallwas assesses H.'s achievement in his "Introduction" to *The Poems of H.: The Lost Poet of Lincoln's Springfield*, suggesting that H. "is the finest poet of his era in the Midwest" (39). H. probably lived in Springfield from the late 1820s to 1833 or 1834. In *Illinois Literature* (65) Hallwas notes that H.'s name might be John Hancock.

**17.** *The Poems of H.*, 81, 82. Subsequent references in the text are from this edition.

**18.** Hallwas, "Introduction," in *The Poems of H.*, 39. While he notes this lack of complexity, Hallwas states that H. can be favorably compared with William Cullen Bryant, John Greenleaf Whittier, Henry Wadsworth Longfellow, James Russell Lowell, and Philip Freneau.

**19.** Hay, *Complete Poetical Works*, 6. Subsequent references in the text are to this edition.

**20.** Holmes, *Poetical Works*, 198. Subsequent references in the text are to this edition.

**21.** See Duberman, *James Russell Lowell*, 63–66, 170–171 and Wagenknecht, *James Russell Lowell*, 57–58, who both call Lowell a "Christian humanist" rather than a romantic.

**22.** Lowell, *Poetical Works*, 90.

**23.** Ibid., 136.

**24.** Wagenknecht, *James Russell Lowell*, 246, note 23. See also Duberman, *James Russell Lowell*, 143 and 423, note 10.

**25.** Cary and Cary, *Poetical Works*, 186–87. Subsequent references in the text are to this edition.

**26.** Kolodny, *The Land before Her*, 158, 161–226.

**27.** See Cora Dolbee's "Kansas and 'The Prairied West' of John G. Whittier," which is a thorough explication of Whittier's connection to Kansas.

**28.** Ibid., 311.

**29.** Whittier, *Complete Poetical Works*, 145. Subsequent references in the text are to this edition.

**30.** The prefatory note to "The Kansas Emigrants" testifies to its popularity: "This song was sent to the first company of emigrants by the poet. 'It is one of the prophecies,' says E. E. Hale, 'for which poets are born, uttered before the event and not after. In absolute hard fact, the song was sung by parties of emigrants, sung when they started, sung as they rode, and sung in the new home'" (317).

Dolbee writes: "Not only was the poem the most quoted through the war years of all Whittier's compositions for the Kansas cause, but it was the most used of all the poems of all writers on the Kansas theme" ("Kansas and 'The Prairied West,'" 323). Dolbee's article also includes reproductions of a holograph copy and two early pamphlet printings of "The Kansas Emigrants."

**31.** Quoted in Dolbee, "Kansas and 'The Prairied West,'" 332.

**32.** Leary, *John Greenleaf Whittier*, 113.

**33.** David Levin, *History as Romantic Art*, 27.

**34.** Quoted in Williams, *Henry Wadsworth Longfellow*, 38.

**35.** Quoted in Wageknecht, *Henry Wadsworth Longfellow*, 133.

**36.** Ibid., 134.

**37.** S. Longfellow, *Life* 1:43.

**38.** Ibid. 2:67.

**39.** The third source was W. I. Kipp's *Early Jesuit Missions in North America* (1847). See also Manning Hawthorne and H. W. L. Dana, *The Origin and Development of Longfellow's "Evangeline."*

**40.** S. Longfellow, *Life* 2:80.

**41.** Quoted in Williams, *Henry Wadsworth Longfellow*, 150.

**42.** H. W. Longfellow, *Complete Poetical Works*, 89–90. Subsequent references in the text are to this edition.

**43.** Newton Arvin claims, "There is a certain suggestion of terror in the prairie landscape. . . . But again it is the beauty of the prairie rather than its fearfulness that dominates" (*Longfellow*, 106). Arvin notes neither the dread nor sorrow associated with the prairie, however, and I disagree that beauty dominates (though the prairie is also beautiful). Most references to the prairies in "Evangeline" are somber and representative of loss.

**44.** See S. Longfellow, *Life* 2:273, 283, and Williams, *Henry Wadsworth Longfellow*, 158. In particular, Longfellow used Schoolcraft's *Algic Researches* (1839); *Oneota; or, Characteristics of the Red Race of America* (1844–45); and *Historical and Statistical Information . . . of the Indian Tribes* (1851–54). He also relied on George Catlin's *Letters and Notes on the Manners, Customs and Condition of the North American Indian* (1841), John Heckewelder's *Transactions of the American Philosophical Society*, vol. 1 (1818), and John Tanner's *A Narrative of the Captivity and Adventures among the Indians* (1830). See Carr, "The Myth of Hiawatha."

**45.** The following give accounts of Longfellow's unrealistic treatment of Indian life: Arvin, *Longfellow*, 154–80; Carr, "The Myth of Hiawatha"; Davis, "How Indian is *Hiawatha?*"; and Thompson, "The Indian Legend of Hiawatha."

**46.** Tichi, "Longfellow's Motives," 549, 551.

**47.** Williams, *Henry Wadsworth Longfellow*, 157.

**48.** I do not wish to suggest that Longfellow's poem is innocent of any political consequences, even though those consequences were most likely unintentional. According to Eric Sundquist, "*Hiawatha* acts out in cultural form the conquest of native life with the native's own complicity." It "ameliorates white conquest, and in [Hiawatha's] death and disappearance he, like the Indians of America, is symbolically absorbed by the West—the Christian eternity, the temporary home of removed Indians, and the ultimate goal of Euro-American destiny" ("The Indian Gallery," 46). See also Helen Carr's "The Myth of Hiawatha," whose more extended argument asserts that the poem's "consoling myth was as essential to the dispossession of the Indian as the raucous racism of the frontiersmen, or the legalistic exclusion of the Indian from natural rights" by the government (74).

**49.** See H. W. Longfellow, *Complete Poetical Works*, 122, 123, 130, 132, 134, 147, 164. I give the page numbers to the prairie references cited in this paragraph to indicate how they are spread throughout the story. Often there are two or more similes that use the prairies on these pages. The page numbers do not include references to the prairies that I discuss later in the chapter.

50. Justus, "The Fireside Poets," 148.

**CHAPTER FOUR. From "Revery" to Nightmare**

1. In *The Undiscovered Continent: Emily Dickinson and the Space of Mind*, Suzanne Juhasz correctly and clearly demonstrates that Dickinson's type of "mental experience," as defined in her poems, "assumes, categorically, that these [mental] events are real" (10). See particularly Juhasz's discussion of Dickinson's "poems about the space of the mind: the undiscovered continent, the landscape of the spirit" (14–27).

Two other book-length studies analyze the quality of Dickinson's imagination. Comparing Dickinson's poetics to Wordsworth's, Keats's, Shelley's, and Emerson's, Joanna Feit Diehl in *Dickinson and the Romantic Imagination* concludes: "Although she shares with them a faith in the sovereignty of the imagination and a belief in its powers, her skepticism—a distrust of nature and insistence upon the primacy of the mind—extends and intensifies one side of a dialectic already shaping Romantic thought" (183). Exploring the "metaphoric-metamorphic structures of [Dickinson's] art," Inder Nath Kher in *The Landscape of Absence: Emily Dickinson's Poetry* concludes: "For Dickinson, the act of poetry is the act of living; the creative process is the way of self-realization which she embodies in her poetic images and symbols. . . . Dickinson's poetic vision . . . is also her vision of life" (1, 271).

About the aphoristic quality of Dickinson's poems, see Juhasz, *The Undiscovered Continent*, 32–35.

When referring to Dickinson's poems, I use Thomas H. Johnson's numbers, as set forth in *The Complete Poems of Emily Dickinson*. Subsequent references in the text are to this edition and cite poem, not page, numbers. The numbers are preceded by a capital *P* to distinguish Dickinson's poems from her letters (see note 7 below).

2. Stevens, *The Palm at the End of the Mind*, 175.

3. It is obvious that Dickinson also investigates in her poetry how knowledge is gained through the senses—especially through sight. Though several poems demonstrate her reliance on vision, "Before I got my eye put out" (P 327) is a representative example. Here the visual perception of "Meadows," "Mountains," "All Forests," and "Stintless Stars" gives the poet ownership of those things. Sight gives ownership, however, not only of the specific meadows, mountains, forests, and stars that she sees, but also of "All Forests," implying those seen and unseen. As is the case with the moor and sea, once one's conscious mind contains knowledge, the knowledge exists independently of the sense perceptions that originally brought it to consciousness.

4. In two other poems Dickinson associates clovers and bees with grassy expanses and suggests themes common to the prairie metaphor. In "It's all I have to bring today—" (P 26) the speaker says that all she can bring her lover is "This, and my heart, and all the fields— / And all the meadows wide—." She summarizes at the end of the poem, "This, and my heart, and all the Bees / Which in the Clover dwell." In the poem "His oriental heresies" (P 1526) "the Bee" fills the metaphysical expanses of "all the Earth and Air" before being attracted to "a Clover plain." Note also the pun on "plain." The word is both noun and adjective, signifying a landscape and the commonness of the clover. This pun is similar to the one in "The Day undressed—Herself—" (P 716), which I discuss later in this chapter.

5. Much has been written about Dickinson's being essentially a metaphoric poet. In his influential study *Emily Dickinson's Poetry*, Robert Weisbuch asserts that Dickinson's poems are analogies. See chapter 2, particularly, in which he writes: "I call Dickinson an analogical poet because analogy suggests an extended equation (*a* is to *b* as *c* is to *d*) carried out by a rigorous logic whose comparisons are always functional and never merely decorative. Further, we may think of metaphor as a complete analogy, in which the progressive logic of associations is buried; conversely, we may think of analogy as a metaphor-in-the-making, in which the associative process calls attention to itself" (13).

Agreeing with Weisbuch, Suzanne Juhasz in *The Undiscovered Continent* also sees Dickinson as a poet of analogy. See chapter 2, particularly, in which she writes: "Through a frequent and thorough use of metaphors based upon a structure of analogy, the interaction between these linguistic opposites [the abstract and concrete] is effected" (51). Helen McNeil in *Emily Dickinson* summarizes her view, also based on Weisbuch's, of Dickinson's use of metaphor:

> Dickinson uses collections of analogies to approximate an issue; her terminology is often highly specific, drawn from precise natural observation or from the terminology of botany, geology, astronomy or dressmaking. Yet her references— her signifieds—are usually either suppressed or left out; there is a denial of the historic dominance of the signified, and a consequent stress upon the poem as investigative or heuristic act. We may never find out what the pearls "mean" in "We play at Paste—" but we soon come to understand the action of learning gem-tactics. (137)

See also McNeil, *Emily Dickinson*, 133–38.

Kher sees Dickinson's poetry as "a primordial metaphor. . . .

Embodying both mythic and existential reality, it points to the center in which the concrete and the intangible meet, in which contraries exist side by side, and in which all the doublenesses of life are encompassed. Its metaphoric structure of reality contains both encounter and resolution, quest and fulfillment, suffering and exhilaration" (*The Landscape of Absence*, 7; see also 47–50).

For a view opposing Weisbush's and Kher's, see E. Miller Budick, *Emily Dickinson and the Life of Language: A Study in Symbolic Poetics*, especially 29–44, 163 f. Budick contends that Kher's and Weisbuch's views "imply a faith, presumably Dickinson's, . . . that through the use of a symbol the artist can identify, represent, and make meaningful and unified elements of a material-spiritual universe; . . . that the artist can make cogent statements about the configuration of the dual cosmos and of the human synthesis of cosmic realities" (36). Budick, on the other hand, argues that "much of Dickinson's poetry is explicitly concerned with exposing the fallacies of various symbolic systems, that at its core Dickinson's poetry, for all its abundant display of symbols, is adamantly critical of many of the strategies we frequently associate with poetic symbolism" (163).

Wendy Barker in *Lunacy of Light: Emily Dickinson and the Experience of Metaphor* characterizes Dickinson's poetry as "shaped by metaphoric clusters" (2–3) that reveal that "this poet wrote keenly aware of her individual talent in relation to the normative tradition preceding and surrounding her, and, through her metaphors, repeatedly and consistently defined herself in opposition to this tradition" (30). Particularly in her metaphors of light and dark, contends Barker, Dickinson subverts the "normative tradition": "Refusing to ignore the blinding resonances of light/dark metaphors that occurred and recurred throughout her culture, Emily Dickinson explored these metaphors, revised them, and finally, transformed them, according to her own 'premises,' her own actual experiences as woman writing" (132–33).

**6.** "Before I got my eye put out" (P 327) uses the word *Meadows* instead of plain or prairie, but the way the word is used in juxtaposition to mountains is similar to the way *plain* is used in "It sifts from Leaden Sieves—" (P 311), "A Tongue—to tell Him I am True!" (P 400), and "The Mountain sat upon the Plain" (P 975). The speaker states,

> Before I got my eye put out
> I liked as well to see—
> As other Creatures, that have Eyes
> And know no other way—

But now, knowing the value of sight, she *sees* differently:

But were it told to me—Today—
That I might have the sky
For mine—I tell you that my Heart
Would split, for size of me—

The Meadows—mine—
The Mountains—mine—
All Forests—Stintless Stars—
As much of Noon as I could take
Between my finite eyes[.]

Surrounding the three images that depict the earth (mountains, meadows, forests) are two images of the sky—the "sky" itself and the "Stintless Stars." As she becomes more profoundly metaphorical, Dickinson uses "Noon" to represent the fullness and brilliance of the sky. Finally, she ends the poem on a spiritual plain, her only company "just my soul." Thus, as she associates the material earth's relationship with the ethereal sky, Dickinson metaphorically conjoins physical and ephemeral existence.

7. When quoting from Dickinson's letters, I use Thomas H. Johnson's numbers, as set forth in *The Letters of Emily Dickinson*. Subsequent references in the text are to this edition and cite letter, not page, numbers. The numbers are preceded by a capital *L* to distinguish the letters from the poems.

8. This poem, like "It sifts from Leaden Sieves—," also relates the prairie metaphor to the poet's art: "No other Art" but prayer, not poetry, for instance—"would do" to communicate with God. See Barbara Antonina Clarke Mossberg, *Emily Dickinson: When a Writer Is a Daughter*, 127.

9. Though Jane Donahue Eberwein in *Dickinson: Strategies of Limitation* states that Dickinson "seemed curiously unmoved by the great westward migration of her countrymen" (109), it is clear that she uses that migration when appropriate to make a metaphor to her own ends.

10. Rebecca Patterson in *Emily Dickinson's Imagery* states that "there is no more erotic poetry in the English language" than Emily Dickinson's (30). While her view is exaggerated as it refers to Dickinson's poetry as a whole, Patterson is correct in noting the sometimes overtly sexual quality of particular Dickinson poems.

See the following poems, which variously depict the sexuality of the bee: P 213, 230, 620, 661, 869, 896, 1224, 1339, 1522, 1526.

11. Bezanson, "Introduction," l.

12. Brodwin, "Melville's *Clarel*," 384.

13. Melville, *Clarel*, 523. Subsequent references in the text are to this edition.

14. Bezanson, "Introduction," l.

15. Bezanson, "Introduction"; Brodwin, "Melville's *Clarel*"; and Shurr, *The Mystery of Iniquity*, 79–123, essentially agree with this summary. See also Kenny, "*Clarel*," 375–406.

16. Buell, "Melville and the Question of American Decolonization," 231.

17. Milder, "The Rhetoric of Melville's *Battle-Pieces*," 199–200.

18. Shurr connects Nathan's spiritual disease with the religious history of America: "Melville recapitulates the American experience in Nathan. He has found the pattern of history: from stern puritanism, to its mellowing as the early colonies expanded, to deism, to the 'Pantheism' of the transcendentalist movement, to the mid-nineteenth-century crisis of belief. That it is a decline, and not merely an evolution, seems clear from the many references to the Fall and Nathan as Adam" (*The Mystery of Iniquity*, 86–87).

19. Bezanson, "Introduction," liv.

20. Melville's use of the White Mountains is noteworthy. Of course, there are echoes from *Moby Dick* in the color white, and there is the convenient irony of a dirty slide of rocks down the pure side of these American mountains. Melville's use of the White Mountains, therefore, is no accident, though he does draw on an "accidental coincidence." Such a slide did occur, in fact, in the White Mountains in 1826. Another interesting aspect of the actual slide is the irony of the Wiley family's attempted escape. Their cabin was left unharmed by the slide because a rock ledge parted the slide around the cabin. The Wileys and their hired hands, nine people in all, were killed when leaving the cabin in an attempt to escape. See Melville, *Clarel*, 569, editor's note.

21. Dimock, *Empire for Liberty*, 7.

22. Melville's poems about art, which appear in his last book of poetry, *Timoleon*, indicate his concern for aesthetics, as do Dickinson's poems about poetry and poets. See "Art" (231) and "The Attic Landscape" (245–46). "In a Garret" voices Melville's discouragement with his abilities to write poetry and to reach an audience:

> Gems and jewels let them heap—
> Wax sumptuous as the Sophi:
> For me, to grapple from Art's deep
> One dripping trophy! (228)

See also Shurr, "Melville's Poems," 351–74.

23. Melville, *Collected Poems*, 226–67. Subsequent references in the text are to this edition.

**24.** See Melville, *Collected Poems*, 473–74, editor's note.

**25.** Bryan C. Short also recognizes the personal quality of *John Marr*, which he sees as Melville's "inward look at his own creative processes" ("Memory's Mint," 42).

**26.** It is interesting to note that the personal and psychological quality of the shifting voice in "Pebbles" makes the sequence resemble some of Dickinson's more puzzling and personal poems.

## CHAPTER FIVE. Reaping the Harvest

**1.** Erkkila, *Whitman*, 83, 86.

**2.** Fussell, *Lucifer in Harness*, 49–55.

**3.** Whitman, *Prose Works, 1892* 1:220. This edition is hereafter cited in the text as *Prose*.

**4.** Whitman, *Leaves of Grass*, 24. This edition is hereafter cited in the text as *LG*.

**5.** Whitman, *The Eighteenth Presidency!*, 27.

**6.** Whitman places the Kansas State Silver Wedding celebration (the Old Settler's Quarter Centennial) in Topeka. Actually, the celebration, to which his party and he were invited, was held on September 15 and 16 at Bismarck Grove, near Lawrence. See Eitner, *Walt Whitman's Western Jaunt*, 3–4, 27–35, 95.

**7.** See, respectively, *Prose* 2:426–33, *Prose* 2:463, and *LG* 746–47.

**8.** Allen, *The Solitary Singer*, 338.

**9.** In their book-length studies of the structure of *Leaves of Grass* both Thomas Edward Crawley (*The Structure of "Leaves of Grass,"* 86–90) and James E. Miller, Jr. (*A Critical Guide to "Leaves of Grass,"* 186–96), argue that "Starting from Paumanok" is an introduction to *Leaves of Grass*. Miller summarizes: "Both the 'Inscriptions' group and 'Starting from Paumanok' serve multiple introductory purposes: they dedicate *Leaves of Grass*; they invoke the appropriate muse; they announce the various major and minor themes; they introduce the images that are to dominate the book; they prepare for and even establish important symbols; they invite intimacy with the reader; and they ask him to join in the experience to come" (189). See also Asselineau, *Evolution* 1:117–19, and Allen, *Handbook*, 95–96, 119–21.

**10.** J. Miller, *Walt Whitman*, 50.

**11.** J. Miller, *Critical Guide*, 186, 197–218.

**12.** Leonard, "The Achievement of Rondure," 79.

**13.** Stephen L. Tanner points out the significance of stargazing in Whitman's *Specimen Days*. He states that the "star-filled sky is unique among the aspects of nature in its *spiritual* influences," and that it is "a symbol of an eternal realm which impinges at all times upon the changing flux of the everyday world" ("Star-Gazing," 159, 158; Tanner's emphasis).

14. It is interesting to note the similarity of diction in this line and in Whitman's letter from the prairies to Anne Gilchrist, November 10, 1879: *"the real America* I find, (& I find that I wasn't realizing it before)—" (*Correspondence* 3:169, Whitman's emphasis).

15. Marx, *The Machine in the Garden*, 222.

16. In addition to the poems mentioned in this chapter, Whitman wrote others specifically about the prairies. "The Prairie-Grass Dividing" is centrally located in the "Calamus" group. It suggests the regenerative, cyclical qualities that are so important to the prairie metaphor, and it suggests the spiritual nature of a manly, "adhesive" love. "O Tan-Faced Prairie-Boy" in "Drum-Taps" recounts the significance of a look exchanged between a veteran soldier and a recruit. The boy's look is spiritually revitalizing for the old veteran. "The Prairie States," the concluding poem of *Autumn Rivulets*, proclaims that America, represented by the prairie states, is the culmination of world history, and as such it is the incarnation of a New Eden.

### CHAPTER SIX. History and Poetry

1. Bassett, *Short History*, v.

2. Nye, "Editor's Introduction," xx. Nye's assessment is firmly based on contemporary reviews of Bancroft, not the least significant of which is one written by Henry Adams in 1875. Even while addressing what he saw as Bancroft's shortcomings, Adams, whose mode of history was more "scientific" as opposed to Bancroft's romantic mode, admits not only to Bancroft's popularity but to his embodying the spirit of his times.

3. Bancroft, *History*, 1, v, 1. Subsequent references in the text are to this edition.

4. Tocqueville, *Democracy in America* 1:3. Subsequent references in the text are to this edition.

5. Flint, *Condensed Geography*, 164; my emphasis. Subsequent references in the text are to this edition.

6. Howe, *Historical Collections*, 8.

7. Rosenthal, "Introduction," vii.

8. Parkman, *The Oregon Trail*, 31–33. Subsequent references in the text are to this edition.

9. Hurt, *Writing Illinois*, 23.

10. See Margaret Dickie's "Dickinson's Discontinuous Lyric Self" in which she claims that for Dickinson the lyric "is a deliberate choice of

self-presentation, expressive of a particular sense of the self (of herself or a self) as shifting, changing, reforming" (538).

**11.** See Ezra Greenspan's *Walt Whitman and the American Reader* for an extended explanation of Whitman's "bringing about the merge between the private and the public" (234).

# WORKS CITED

Allen, Gay Wilson. *The New Walt Whitman Handbook*. New York: New York University Press, 1986.

———. *The Solitary Singer: A Critical Biography of Walt Whitman*. Chicago: University of Chicago Press, 1985.

Anderson, Douglas. "Presence and Place in Emily Dickinson's Poetry." *New England Quarterly* 57 (1984): 205–24.

Antelyes, Peter. *Tales of Adventurous Enterprise: Washington Irving and the Poetics of Western Expansion*. New York: Columbia University Press, 1990.

Arms, George. *The Fields Were Green: A New View of Bryant, Whittier, Holmes, Lowell, and Longfellow with a Selection of Their Poems*. Stanford, Calif.: Stanford University Press, 1953.

Arvin, Newton. *Longfellow: His Life and Work*. Boston: Little, Brown, 1963.

Asselineau, Roger. *The Evolution of Walt Whitman: The Creation of a Personality*. 2 vols. Cambridge, Mass.: Belknap Press, 1960.

Bachelard, Gaston. *The Poetics of Space*. Translated by Maria Jolas. New York: Orion, 1964.

Bancroft, George. *History of the Colonization of the United States*. . . . 23d ed. Vol. 1. Boston: Little, Brown, 1870.

Barker, Wendy. *Lunacy of Light: Emily Dickinson and the Experience of Metaphor*. Carbondale: Southern Illinois University Press, 1987.

Bassett, John Spencer. *A Short History of the United States*. 1913. New York: Macmillan, 1919.

Baxter, David J. "The Dilemma of Progress: Bryant's Continental Vision." In Stanley Brodwin and Michael D'Innocenzo, eds., *William Cullen Bryant and His America*, 13–25. New York: AMS, 1983.

———. "William Cullen Bryant: Illinois Landowner." *Western Illinois Regional Studies* 1 (1978): 1–14.

Bezanson, Walter E. Introduction. In Herman Melville, *Clarel*, ix-cxvii. New York: Hendricks House, 1960.

Billington, Ray Allen, and Martin Ridge. *Westward Expansion: A History of the American Frontier*. 5th ed. New York: Macmillan, 1982.

Booher, Edwin R. "The Garden Myth in 'The Prairies.'" *Western Illinois Regional Studies* 1 (1978): 15–26.

Bowden, Mary Weatherspoon. *Washington Irving*. Boston: Twayne, 1981.

Brodwin, Stanley. "Herman Melville's *Clarel:* An Existential Gospel." *PMLA* 86 (1971): 375–87.

Brodwin, Stanley and Michael D'Innocenzo, eds. *William Cullen Bryant and His America: Centennial Conference Proceedings, 1878–1978*. New York: AMS, 1983.

Brown, Charles H. *William Cullen Bryant*. New York: Scribner's, 1971.

Bryant, John Howard. *Poems, Written from Youth to Old Age, 1824–1884*. Princeton, Ill.: T. P. Streeter, 1885.

Bryant, William Cullen. *The Letters of William Cullen Bryant*. Edited by William Cullen Bryant II and Thomas G. Voss. 4 vols. to date. New York: Fordham University Press, 1975–85.

———. *Poems*. Boston: Russell, Odiorne, and Metcalf, 1834.

———. *Poems*. New York: Harper and Brothers, 1836.

———. *Poems*. 2 vols. New York: D. Appleton, 1862.

———. *The Poems of William Cullen Bryant*. New York: D. Appleton, 1876.

———. *The Poetical Works of William Cullen Bryant*. Edited by Parke Godwin. 2 vols. 1883. New York: Russell and Russell, 1967.

———. "The Prairies." *The Knickerbocker: or, New-York Monthly Magazine* 2 (December 1833): 410–13.

———. *The Prose Writings of William Cullen Bryant*. Edited by Parke Godwin. 2 vols. 1884. New York: Russell and Russell, 1964.

———, ed. *Selections from the American Poets*. New York: Harper, 1874.

Bryant, William Cullen, and Sydney Howard Gay. *A Popular History of the United States, from the First Discovery of the Western Hemisphere by the Northmen, to the End of the First Century of the Union of the States*. 4 vols. New York: Scribner's, 1878.

Bryant, William Cullen, II. "Poetry and Painting: A Love Affair of Long Ago." *American Quarterly* 22 (1970): 859–82.

Budick, E. Miller. *Emily Dickinson and The Life of Language: A Study in Symbolic Poetics*. Baton Rouge: Louisiana State University Press, 1985.

Buell, Lawrence. "Melville and the Question of American Decolonization." *American Literature* 64 (1992): 215–37.

Cameron, Sharon. *Lyric Time: Dickinson and the Limits of Genre*. Baltimore: Johns Hopkins University Press, 1979.

Carr, Helen. "The Myth of Hiawatha." *Literature and History* 12 (1986): 58–78.

Cary, Alice, and Phoebe Cary. *The Poetical Works of Alice and Phoebe Cary, with a Memorial of Their Lives.* Boston: Houghton Mifflin, 1881.

Cassirer, Ernst. *Mythical Thought.* Vol. 2 of *The Philosophy of Symbolic Forms.* Edited by Ralph Manheim. New Haven: Yale University Press, 1955.

Charvat, William. *The Profession of Authorship in America, 1800–1870.* Edited by Matthew J. Bruccoli. Columbus: Ohio State University Press, 1968.

Coggeshall, William Turner. *The Poets and Poetry of the West.* 1860. New York: Arno, 1975.

Cracroft, Richard H. *Washington Irving: The Western Works.* Western Writers Series, no. 14. Boise: Boise State University, 1974.

Crawley, Thomas Edward. *The Structure of "Leaves of Grass."* Austin: University of Texas Press, 1970.

Dahl, Curtis. "Mound-Builders, Mormons, and William Cullen Bryant." *New England Quarterly* 34 (1961): 178–90.

Davis, Rose M. "How Indian is *Hiawatha?*" *Midwest Folklore* 7 (1957): 5–25.

Dickens, Charles. *American Notes for General Circulation.* New York: Penguin, 1985.

Dickie, Margaret. "Dickinson's Discontinuous Lyric Self." *American Literature* 60 (1988): 537–53.

Dickinson, Emily. *The Complete Poems of Emily Dickinson.* Edited by Thomas H. Johnson. Boston: Little, Brown, 1960.

———. *The Letters of Emily Dickinson.* Edited by Thomas H. Johnson and Theodora Ward. 3 vols. Cambridge, Mass.: Belknap Press, 1958.

Diehl, Joanna Feit. *Dickinson and the Romantic Imagination.* Princeton, N.J.: Princeton University Press, 1981.

Dimock, Wai-chee. *Empire for Liberty: Melville and the Poetics of Individualism.* Princeton, N.J.: Princeton University Press, 1989.

Dolbee, Cora. "Kansas and 'The Prairied West' of John G. Whittier." *Essex Institute Historical Collections,* October 1945, 307–47.

Dondore, Dorothy Anne. *The Prairie and the Making of Middle America: Four Centuries of Description.* Cedar Rapids, Iowa: Torch Press, 1926.

Donoghue, Denis. *Connoisseurs of Chaos: Ideas of Order in Modern American Poetry.* New York: Columbia University Press, 1984.

Duberman, Martin. *James Russell Lowell.* Boston: Houghton Mifflin, 1966.

Eberwein, Jane Donahue. *Dickinson: Strategies of Limitation.* Amherst: University of Massachusetts Press, 1985.

Eby, Cecil D., Jr. "Bryant's 'The Prairies': Notes on Date and Text." *Papers of the Bibliographical Society of America* 56 (1962): 356–57.

Eby, Edwin Harold. *A Concordance of Walt Whitman's "Leaves of Grass" and Selected Prose Writings*. Seattle: University of Washington Press, 1955.

Eitner, Walter H. "Some Further Autograph Notes of Whitman's 1879 Western Trip." *Walt Whitman Review* 26 (1980): 18–22.

———. *Walt Whitman's Western Jaunt*. Lawrence: Regents Press of Kansas, 1981.

Emerson, Ralph Waldo. *Essays: Second Series*. Vol. 3 of *The Collected Works of Ralph Waldo Emerson*. Cambridge, Mass.: Belknap Press, 1983.

———. *Letters and Social Aims*. Vol. 8 of *The Complete Works of Ralph Waldo Emerson*. Centenary Ed. Boston: Riverside Press, 1904.

———. *Nature, Addresses, and Lectures*. Vol. 1 of *The Collected Works of Ralph Waldo Emerson*. Cambridge, Mass.: Belknap Press, 1971.

Engel, Bernard F., and Patricia W. Julius. *A New Voice for a New People: Midwestern Poetry, 1800–1910*. Lanham, Md.: University Press of America, 1985.

Erkkila, Betsy. *Whitman the Political Poet*. New York: Oxford University Press, 1989.

Ferguson, Robert A. "William Cullen Bryant: The Creative Context of the Poet." *New England Quarterly* 53 (1980): 431–63.

Field, Matthew. *Matt Field on the Santa Fe Trail*. Edited by John E. Sunder. Collected by Clyde Porter and Mea Reed Porter. Norman: University of Oklahoma Press, 1960.

Flanagan, John T. "Poetic Voices in the Early Middle West." *Centennial Review* 24 (1980): 269–83.

Flint, Timothy. *A Condensed Geography and History of the Western States, or the Mississippi Valley*. Vol. 1. 1828. Gainesville, Fla.: Scholar's Facsimilies, 1970.

Free, William J. "William Cullen Bryant on Nationalism, Imitation, and Originality in Poetry." *Studies in Philology* 66 (1969): 672–87.

Frost, Robert. *The Poetry of Robert Frost*. Edited by Edward Connery Lathem. New York: Holt, Rinehart, and Winston, 1969.

Fussell, Edwin. *Frontier: American Literature and the American West*. Princeton, N.J.: Princeton University Press, 1965.

———. *Lucifer in Harness: American Meter, Metaphor, and Diction*. Princeton, N.J.: Princeton University Press, 1973.

Gelpi, Albert. *The Tenth Muse: The Psyche of the American Poet*. Cambridge, Mass.: Harvard University Press, 1975.

Gilbert, Sandra, and Susan Gubar. *The Madwoman in the Attic*. New Haven, Conn.: Yale University Press, 1979.

Godwin, Parke. *A Biography of William Cullen Bryant, with Extracts from His Private Correspondence*. 2 vols. 1883. New York: Russell and Russell, 1967.

Greenspan, Ezra. *Walt Whitman and the American Reader*. Cambridge and New York: Cambridge University Press, 1990.

Griswold, Rufus Wilmot. *The Poets and Poetry of America*. Philadelphia: Carey and Hart, 1848.

H. *The Poems of H.: The Lost Poet of Lincoln's Springfield*. Edited by John E. Hallwas. Peoria, Ill.: Ellis Press, 1982.

Haight, Gordon S. *Mrs. Sigourney: The Sweet Singer of Hartford*. New Haven, Conn.: Yale University Press, 1930.

Hall, Donald. "Whittier." *Texas Quarterly* 3, no. 3 (1960): 165–74.

Hallwas, John E., ed. *Illinois Literature: The Nineteenth Century*. Macomb, Ill.: Heritage Press, 1986.

———. Introduction. In *The Poems of H*. Peoria, Ill.: Ellis Press, 1982.

———. "The Poetry of John Howard Bryant." *MidAmerica* 7 (1980): 27–39.

———. "The Varieties of Humor in John Hay's Pike County Ballads." *MidAmerica* 5 (1978): 7–18.

Hawthorne, Manning, and H. W. L. Dana. *The Origin and Development of Longfellow's "Evangeline."* Portland, Maine: n.p., 1947.

Hay, John. *The Complete Poetical Works of John Hay*. Household Ed. Boston: Houghton Mifflin, 1917.

Herringshaw, Thomas W., ed. *Local and National Poets of America*. Chicago: American Publishers Association, 1890.

Hill, Murray Gardner. "Some of Longfellow's Sources for the Second Part of *Evangeline*." *PMLA* 31 (1916): 161–80.

Hindus, Milton, ed. *Walt Whitman: The Critical Heritage*. New York: Barnes and Noble, 1971.

Holmes, Oliver Wendell. *The Poetical Works of Oliver Wendell Holmes*. Cambridge Ed. Boston: Houghton Mifflin, 1975.

Howe, Henry. *Historical Collections of the Great West*. Vol. 1. Cincinnati: Henry Howe, E. Morgan, 1854.

Hubach, Robert R. "Western Newspaper Accounts of Whitman's 1879 Trip to the West." *Walt Whitman Review* 18 (1972): 56–62.

Hurt, James. *Writing Illinois: The Prairie, Lincoln, and Chicago*. Urbana: University of Illinois Press, 1992.

Irving, Washington. *A Tour on the Prairies*. Edited by John Francis McDermott. Norman: University of Oklahoma Press, 1962.

Jehlen, Myra. *American Incarnation: The Individual, the Nation, and the Continent*. Cambridge, Mass.: Harvard University Press, 1986.

Johnson, Linck C. "The Design of Walt Whitman's *Specimen Days*." *Walt Whitman Review* 21 (1975): 3–14.

Johnson, Thomas H. *Emily Dickinson: An Interpretive Biography*. New York: Atheneum, 1976.

Juhasz, Suzanne. "'To Make a Prairie': Language and Form in Emily Dickinson's Poems about Mental Experience." *Ball State University Forum* 21 (1980): 12–25.

———. "The 'Undiscovered Continent': Emily Dickinson and the Space of Mind." *Missouri Review* 3, no. 1 (1979): 86–97.

———. *The Undiscovered Continent: Emily Dickinson and the Space of Mind.* Bloomington: Indiana University Press, 1983.

Justus, James H. "The Fireside Poets: Hearthside Values and the Language of Care." In *Nineteenth-Century American Poetry,* edited by A. Robert Lee, 146–65. London: Vision; Totawa, N.J.: Barnes and Noble, 1985.

Kehler, Joel R. "A Typologial Reading of 'Passage to India.'" *ESQ: A Journal of the American Renaissance* 23 (1977): 123–29.

Kenny, Vincent. *"Clarel."* In *A Companion to Melville Studies,* edited by John Bryant, 375–406. New York: Greenwood Press, 1986.

Kher, Inder Nath. *The Landscape of Absence: Emily Dickinson's Poetry.* New Haven, Conn.: Yale University Press, 1974.

Kime, Wayne. "The Author as Professional: Washington Irving's 'Rambling Anecdotes' of the West." In *Critical Essays on Washington Irving,* edited by Ralph M. Aderman, 237–53. Boston: G. K. Hall, 1990.

Kirk, G. S. *Myth: Its Meaning and Functions in Ancient and Other Cultures.* London and Berkeley: Cambridge University Press and University of California Press, 1973.

Kolodny, Annette. *The Land before Her: Fantasy and Experience of the American Frontier, 1630–1860.* Chapel Hill: University of North Carolina Press, 1984.

———. *The Lay of the Land: Metaphor as Experience and History in American Life and Letters.* Chapel Hill: University of North Carolina Press, 1975.

———. "Letting Go Our Grand Obsessions: Notes toward a New Literary History of the American Frontiers." *American Literature* 64 (1992): 1–18.

Kribbs, Jayne K., ed. *Critical Essays on John Greenleaf Whittier.* Boston: G. K. Hall, 1980.

Kuebrich, David. "Whitman's Politics: Poetry and Democracy." *Bucknell Review* 23, no. 2 (1977): 116–30.

Lawrence, D. H. *Studies in Classic American Literature.* New York: Penguin, 1981.

Lawson-Peebles, Robert. *Landscapes and Written Expression in Revolutionary America: The World Turned Upside Down.* New York: Cambridge University Press, 1988.

Leary, Lewis. *John Greenleaf Whittier*. New York: Twayne, 1961.

Leonard, James S. "The Achievement of Rondure in 'Passage to India.'" *Walt Whitman Review* 26 (1980): 129–38.

Levin, David. *History as Romantic Art: Bancroft, Prescott, Motley, and Parkman*. Stanford, Calif.: Stanford University Press, 1959.

Levin, Samuel R. *Metaphoric Worlds: Conceptions of a Romantic Nature*. New Haven, Conn.: Yale University Press, 1988.

Lewis, Meriwether, and William Clark. *The History of the Lewis and Clark Expedition*. Edited by Elliot Coues. 3 vols. Francis P. Harper, 1893. New York: Dover, n.d.

Longfellow, Henry Wadsworth. *The Complete Poetical Works of Henry Wadsworth Longfellow*. Cambridge Ed. Boston: Houghton Mifflin, 1917.

Longfellow, Samuel. *Life of Henry Wadsworth Longfellow, with Extracts from His Journals and Correspondence*. 3 vols. 1891. New York: Greenwood Press, 1969.

Lowell, James Russell. *The Poetical Works of James Russell Lowell*. Cambridge Ed. Boston: Houghton Mifflin, 1978.

McDermott, John Francis. Introductory Essay. In Washington Irving, *A Tour on the Prairies*, xv-xxxii. Norman: University of Oklahoma Press, 1962.

McDowell, Tremaine. Introduction. In *William Cullen Bryant: Representative Selections*. New York: American, 1935.

McLean, Albert F., Jr. "Progress and Dissolution in Bryant's Poetry." In Stanley Brodwin and Michael D'Innocenzo, eds., *William Cullen Bryant and His America*, 155–66. New York: AMS, 1983.

———. *William Cullen Bryant*. New York: Twayne, 1964.

McNeil, Helen. *Emily Dickinson*. New York: Virago/Pantheon Books, 1986.

Marx, Leo. *The Machine in the Garden: Technology and the Pastoral Ideal in America*. New York: Galaxy, 1967.

Matthiessen, F. O. *American Renaissance: Art and Expression in the Age of Emerson and Whitman*. New York: Oxford University Press, 1962.

Melville, Herman. *Clarel: A Poem and a Pilgrimage in the Holy Land*. New York: Hendricks House, 1960.

———. *Collected Poems of Herman Melville*. Edited by Howard P. Vincent. Chicago: Packard, 1947.

Milder, Robert. "The Rhetoric of Melville's *Battle-Pieces*." *Nineteenth-Century Literature* 44 (1989): 173–200.

Miller, Edwin Haviland, ed. *A Century of Whitman Criticism*. Bloomington: Indiana University Press, 1969.

———. *Walt Whitman's Poetry: A Psychological Journey*. New York: New York University Press, 1968.

Miller, James E., Jr. *A Critical Guide to "Leaves of Grass."* Chicago: University of Chicago Press, 1957.

———. *Walt Whitman.* Boston: Twayne, 1962.

Miller, Perry. *Errand into the Wilderness.* Cambridge: Harvard University Press, 1956.

Miller, Ralph N. "Nationalism in Bryant's 'The Prairies.'" *American Literature* 21 (1949): 227–32.

Millward, Celia, and Cecelia Tichi. "Whatever Happened to *Hiawatha*?" *Genre* 6 (1973): 313–32.

Mossberg, Barbara Antonina Clarke. *Emily Dickinson: When a Writer is a Daughter.* Bloomington: Indiana University Press, 1982.

———. "'Everyone Else Is Prose': Emily Dickinson's Lack of Community Spirit." In Paul J. Ferlazzo, ed., *Critical Essays on Emily Dickinson,* 223–38. Boston: G. K. Hall, 1984.

Newlin, Paul A. "*The Prairie* and 'The Prairies': Cooper's and Bryant's Views of Manifest Destiny." In Stanley Brodwin and Michael D'Innocenzo, eds., *William Cullen Bryant and His America,* 27–38. New York: AMS, 1983.

Nichol, John W. "Melville and the Midwest." *PMLA* 66 (1951): 613–25.

Nye, Russel B. "Editor's Introduction." In George Bancroft, *The History of the Colonization of the United States.* Chicago: University of Chicago Press, 1966.

Olson, Steve. "A Perverted Poetics: Bryant's and Emerson's Concern for a Developing American Literature." *American Transcendental Quarterly* 61 (October 1986): 15–21.

———. "William Cullen Bryant's View of Prairie America's Conflicting Values." *North Dakota Quarterly* 53, no. 4 (1985): 35–43.

Parkman, Francis. *The Oregon Trail.* 1849. Chicago: John C. Winston, 1931.

Patterson, Rebecca. *Emily Dickinson's Imagery.* Edited by Margaret H. Freeman. Amherst: University of Massachusetts Press, 1979.

Paulding, J[ames] K[irke]. *The Backwoodsman: A Poem.* Philadelphia: M. Thomas, 1818.

Pearce, Roy Harvey. *The Continuity of American Poetry.* Princeton, N.J.: Princeton University Press, 1961.

Piasecki, Bruce. "Whitman's 'Estimate of Nature' in *Democratic Vistas.*" *Walt Whitman Review* 27 (1981): 101–12.

Poe, Edgar Allan. "The Philosophy of Composition." In Nina Baym et al., eds., *The Norton Anthology of American Literature,* 3d ed., 1:1459–67. New York: Norton, 1989.

Pound, Ezra. *Selected Poems.* New York: New Directions, 1957.

Ricoeur, Paul. *The Rule of Metaphor: Multi-disciplinary Studies of the Creation*

*of Meaning in Language*. Translated by Robert Czerny. Toronto:
University of Toronto Press, 1977.

Ringe, Donald A. *The Pictorial Mode: Space and Time in the Art of Bryant, Irving, and Cooper*. Lexington: University Press of Kentucky, 1971.

Rosenthal, Bernard. Introduction. In Timothy Flint, *A Condensed Geography and History of the Western States* 1:v–xii. Gainesville, Fla.: Scholar's Facsimiles, 1970.

Rusk, Ralph Leslie. *The Literature of the Middle Western Frontier*. 2 vols. New York: Columbia University Press, 1925.

Schyberg, Frederik. *Walt Whitman*. Translated by Evie Allison Allen. New York: Columbia University Press, 1951.

Sewall, Richard B. *The Life of Emily Dickinson*. New York: Farrar, Straus and Giroux, 1980.

Short, Bryan C. "Memory's Mint: Melville's Parable of the Imagination in *John Marr and Other Sailors*." *Essays in Arts and Sciences* 15 (1986): 31–42.

Shurr, William H. "Melville's Poems: The Late Agenda." In *A Companion to Melville Studies*, edited by John Bryant, 351–74. New York: Greenwood Press, 1986.

———. *The Mystery of Iniquity: Melville as Poet, 1857–1891*. Lexington: University Press of Kentucky, 1972.

Sigourney, Lydia Huntley. *Select Poems*. 5th ed. Philadelphia: E. C. and J. Biddle, 1847.

———. *The Western Home, and Other Poems*. Philadelphia: Parry and Mc-Millan, 1854.

Silber, Robert Bernard. "William Cullen Bryant's 'Lectures on Mythology.'" Ph.D. diss., State University of Iowa (University of Iowa), 1962.

Slotkin, Richard. "Myth and Production of History." In Sacvan Bercovitch and Myra Jehlen, eds., *Ideology and Classic American Literature*, 70–90. Cambridge: Cambridge University Press, 1986.

Smith, Henry Nash. *Virgin Land: The American West as Symbol and Myth*. Cambridge, Mass.: Harvard University Press, 1950.

Stein, William Bysshe. *The Poetry of Melville's Late Years: Time, History, Myth, and Religion*. Albany: State University of New York Press, 1970.

Steinbrink, Jeffery. "'To Span Vast Realms of Space and Time': Whitman's Vision of History." *Walt Whitman Review* 24 (1978): 45–62.

Stevens, Wallace. *The Palm at the End of the Mind*. New York: Vintage Books, 1971.

Stibitz, E. Earle. *Illinois Poets: A Selection*. Carbondale: Southern Illinois University Press, 1968.

Sundquist, Eric J. "The Indian Gallery: Antebellum Literature and the Containment of the American Indian." In Beverly R. Voloshin, ed., *American Literature, Culture, and Ideology: Essays in Memory of Henry Nash Smith*, 37–64. New York: Peter Lang, 1990.

Tanner, Stephen L. "Star-Gazing in Whitman's *Specimen Days*." *Walt Whitman Review* 19 (1973): 158–61.

Thompson, Stith. "The Indian Legend of Hiawatha." *PMLA* 37 (1922): 128–40.

Tichi, Cecelia. "Longfellow's Motives for the Structure of 'Hiawatha.'" *American Literature* 42 (1971): 548–53.

———. *New World, New Earth: Environmental Reform in American Literature from the Puritans through Whitman*. New Haven, Conn.: Yale University Press, 1979.

Tilton, Eleanor M. *Amiable Autocrat: A Biography of Dr. Oliver Wendell Holmes*. New York: Henry Schuman, 1947.

Tocqueville, Alexis de. *Democracy in America*. 1835, 1840. Translated by Henry Reeve. Rev. ed. 2 vols. New York: P. F. Collier, 1900.

Tuan, Yi-Fu. *Topophilia: A Study of Environmental Perception, Attitudes, and Values*. Englewood Cliffs, N.J.: Prentice-Hall, 1974.

Turco, Lewis Putnam. *Visions and Revisions of American Poetry*. Fayetteville: University of Arkansas Press, 1986.

Turner, Frederick Jackson. "The Significance of the Frontier in American History." In George Rogers Taylor, ed., *The Turner Thesis: Concerning the Role of the Frontier in American History*. 3d ed. Lexington, Mass.: D. C. Heath, 1972.

Turner, Mark. *Death Is the Mother of Beauty: Mind, Metaphor, Criticism*. Chicago: University of Chicago Press, 1987.

Vincent, Howard P. Introduction. In Herman Melville, *Collected Poems*, vii-xii. Chicago: Packard, 1947.

Wagenknecht, Edward. *Henry Wadsworth Longfellow: Portrait of an American Humanist*. New York: Oxford University Press, 1966.

———. *James Russell Lowell: Portrait of a Many-Sided Man*. New York: Oxford University Press, 1971.

———. *John Greenleaf Whittier: A Portrait in Paradox*. New York: Oxford University Press, 1967.

———. *Longfellow: A Full-Length Portrait*. New York: Longmans, Green, 1955.

Wallace, Anthony F. C. "Prelude to Disaster: The Course of Indian-White Relations Which Led to the Black Hawk War of 1832." In Ellen M. Whitney, ed., *The Black Hawk War, 1831–1832* 1:1–51. Springfield: Illinois State Historical Library, 1970.

Warren, Robert Penn. "John Greenleaf Whittier: Poetry as Experience."

In *John Greenleaf Whittier's Poetry: An Appraisal and a Selection*, 3–
61. Minneapolis: University of Minnesota Press, 1971.

Weaver, J. E. *North American Prairie*. Lincoln, Neb.: Johnsen, 1954.

Weisbuch, Robert. *Emily Dickinson's Poetry*. Chicago: University of Chicago Press, 1975.

White, Richard. *"It's Your Misfortune and None of My Own": A History of the American West*. Norman: University of Oklahoma Press, 1991.

Whitman, Walt. *The Correspondence*. Edited by Edwin Haviland Miller. 5 vols. New York: New York University Press, 1961–69.

———. *Daybooks and Notebooks*. Edited by William White. 3 vols. New York: New York University Press, 1978.

———. *The Eighteenth Presidency!* Edited by Edward F. Grier. Lawrence: University of Kansas Press, 1956.

———. *Leaves of Grass* Edited by Harold W. Blodgett and Sculley Bradley. Comprehensive Reader's Edition. New York: New York University Press, 1965.

———. *Prose Works, 1892*. Edited by Floyd Stovall. 2 vols. New York: New York University Press, 1963–64.

———. *The Uncollected Poetry and Prose of Walt Whitman*. Edited by Emory Holloway. 2 vols. New York: Peter Smith, 1932.

Whittier, John Greenleaf. *The Complete Poetical Works of Whittier*. Cambridge Ed. Boston: Houghton Mifflin, 1894.

Williams, Cecil B. *Henry Wadsworth Longfellow*. New York: Twayne, 1964.

# INDEX